HOW TO LIVE UP

BY THE POWER OF ENCOURAGEMENT

CLAUDIA PORTER

Liberty Trades Publishing

Colorado, USA

Joy to you!
Claudia Porter

Printed by LIBERTY TRADES PUBLISHING, in the United States of America

Contents

What Readers are Saying

"Claudia Porter knows people! Claudia Porter knows the gospel and the king who offers His kingdom to those hurting and trapped in the chains of negative labels or as she says, "soul tattoos." Claudia understands the way out of bondage and the light in the darkness that leads the way to freedom. Claudia has the amazing ability to write with clarity and simplicity when the material she is covering is complex. Her examples engage us in the areas we are familiar with, to help us understand dynamics that may be abstract. She is a gifted writer and teacher and her book is a blessing. Perhaps the greatest compliment a fellow writer can say about Claudia is that she just does not know about God, but knows God. She is a disciple who studies the word and applies it, as is made plain in this book. She is not just a teacher of God's word but a disciple of Jesus. Not just a hearer of the word but a doer who knows the Caller. My firm belief is that you will greatly benefit by reading and working on the exercises in each chapter of *How to Live Up*. Seek Him and enjoy this book."

Randy Reynolds, LPC, Pastor, Counselor, Author, and Community Developer

Finally! This is something *everyone* can do to truly make a positive difference in a world that is full of hurt. Here's to the power of encouragement!!! I'm sooooo tired of reading and hearing about everything that's wrong and awful. Let's start getting involved in the lives of others through encouragement! Let's watch people rise from the ashes of their beaten-down lives.

Ellen DeVoss, Community Leader

"It has been my pleasure to watch Claudia live out her convictions concerning the power of encouragement for many years. She truly knows how to lift the spirits of those around her with a carefully spoken word, a gentle touch, a compassionate glance, or a kind deed. Whether leading worship, sharing a story of God's powerful working in her life, offering a friend a cup of soothing hot tea, or simply holding a hurting friend, she has been "Jesus with skin on" for all who know her. A wise person would do well to read her book and seek to follow her instruction and example."

Denie Dalton, Veteran Educator

Little did I know when I first heard Claudia's unique message on JOY, that this lesson would guide me into a more emotionally healthy place for decades of ministry to come. Claudia's gift to creatively explain biblical truths shines ever so brightly in her new book, HOW TO LIVE UP. *Reader beware!* Your thoughts will be challenged – and you'll confront a new viewpoint to improve those unhealthy "downer days" and ugly, negative moods we all often battle and be *unstoppable* in your divine assignments. This book would be my *top pick* for your next small group study, to serve as a manual of encouragement among colleagues, family, friends, or churchmates! HOW TO LIVE UP also belongs on every counselor's reading list, and should be part of women's ministries, youth groups, and pre-marital preparation to equip newlyweds before their big day.

Nancy Lueckhof, Christian Frontier Ministries, Author of SULUAN, Motivational Speaker

"How to Live Up is a right now message for the body of Christ. I have known Claudia Porter for over 20 years- as a worship leader, Bible teacher, missionary, conference speaker, and friend. She is one of the wisest, most godly, most consistently UP people I have ever met. I enthusiastically recommend this book to anyone who wants to be an ENCOURAGED ENCOURAGER!"

Rev. Charles Reischman, Founder Joshua Force

FOREWORD

This book is the Life Message of my treasured friend of almost 40 years.

Where would I be if Claudia Porter had not come into my life? My late husband Dave and I were newbies in leading a local church. Some would compliment me on my speaking efforts by calling me "prophetic."

After watching Claudia speak publicly and interact with people one-on-one in such a positive and encouraging way, I realized I was "mean" in comparison. And so began my journey of gleaning from this dynamic woman, especially learning the power of encouragement.

Eventually, Claudia and I ministered together for ten years through an organization we founded, *Women Embracing the World*, bringing encouragement to American women who were missionaries in foreign lands. We brought them to our Colorado-based WEW

Conference to infuse them with desperately needed encouragement-strength spirit, soul, and body. They returned to their assignments uplifted and refueled.

Along with our husbands, we planted a church together. We traveled the world together—to Russia, Great Britain, Uganda and Kenya, East Africa.

Because of our travel to England, Claudia made contact with people who would help her found a home for abandoned babies in Uganda, where in ten years of operation, over seventy babies have been rescued, cared for, and many placed into loving Forever Families. Then she turned her attention to lifting the suffering of the children living in the slums of Nairobi and spearheaded the building of an accessible Christian school for several hundreds of them.

Thank you, Claudia, for being willing to assume the arduous task of writing this book so that millions more can benefit from your life of encouragement—just as I have for all these years!

Dr. Bonnie Duell
Founder and Apostle, Faith Ministries Network
Founder and Pastor, Faith Ministries Church, Denver, Colorado USA

I

THE UPLIFTING POWER WE ALL NEED

There are high spots in most of our lives
and most of them have come about
through encouragement from someone else.
I don't care how great, how famous,
how successful a man or woman may be,
each hunger for applause.
–George Adams

Nobody wants to live a mediocre life. Mediocre is a French

word that means "halfway up the hill" or "unremarkable." Why do we settle for mediocre? Most of us hope that our lives will be joyful and satisfying and include some notable and worthy accomplishments. We have an inner sense that there is a *uniquely designed* assignment and story for our lives to express. And there is! But uphill challenges, pandemics, and other disappointments can deflate our dreams and bully us back to "oh-well" land.

It is only when we dare to take the plunge out of "down-living" and become a student of divine enCOURAGEment that we will thrive. Every great accomplishment ordained by our Creator *requires* that we learn how to draw from Him the courage *necessary* to fulfill it.

Chalkdust Applause

One beautiful, Colorado morning I power-walked along my usual exercise track around a lake, and I noticed a red, heart-shaped sign that said, "Avon Breast Cancer Walk." Although the event occurred several days before, ruby heart chalk-drawn images remained along the pathway. "That's cool," I thought, and I sadly remembered several friends I'd known over the years who had suffered from the scourge of cancer.

As I paused for a moment to wipe a bead of sweat from my brow, my eye caught something colorful on the ground just beyond me. Someone had used pastel sidewalk chalk to write a message in giant letters. It said, "*Way to go, walkers!*" Impressed, I walked a little further and discovered *another* chalk message. "*You can do it!*" Then, more encouraging "chalk cheers" shouted up to me from all along the path. "*We're proud of you!*" "*Almost there!*" "*Showers ahead!*" These encouraging etchings, had hands and voices raised in applause, inspiring any weary walkers, reminding them of the *purpose* of the walk and to *keep going.*

Almost unconsciously, my gait picked up, and my joy increased as I strained to see the *next* motivating message! Even though I wasn't one of the official cancer walkers, I felt connected to them, excited to walk upon this now-sacred passageway. *A light turned on in my mind.* The sponsors of this event realized a *vital* secret about something *all* "walkers" need. These soft-hued, chalkdust praises etched on the ground fueled these walkers to the finish line. Everyone traveling this rocky path of life requires a *consistent infusion of encouragement* to keep pressing onward. But very few know where to get it. Far more substantial than chalk dust, an unlimited source of divine realities and encouragement await us in the pages ahead.

Everyone traveling this rocky path of life requires a consistent infusion of encouragement to keep pressing onward. But very few know where to get it.

What is enCOURAGEment?

Picture what the literal definition of each part of the word could mean in your life.

Spirit-infused encouragement empowers us with heart-strength to venture, persevere, and resist opposition in order to fulfill our divine purpose and see concrete results.

–EN: "*To provide with and cause to have*"

–COURAGE: "*Heart-strength to venture, persevere and resist opposition, empowerment to achieve one's ends.*"

–MENT: "*a concrete result.*"

In other words, the definition paraphrased becomes:

–Spirit-infused "encouragement" empowers us with heart-strength to venture, persevere, and resist opposition to fulfill our divine purpose and see concrete results.

The potential is *exciting*. This life-boosting, genuine encouragement will propel us beyond the black-hole gravitational pull of fear and depression and thrust us into orbit around the bright star of our God-given destiny. These pages of profound truths and stories from scripture and my own experiences are written to become your "handbook-into-joy". Each chapter illustrates a practical truth that *when applied*, will energize *your* expedition upward. And the truth is, we are starting from a supernaturally lifted position.

BONUS BOOSTER

"And God raised us up with Christ and seated us with Him in the heavenly realms in Christ Jesus, in order that in the coming ages He might display the surpassing riches of His grace, demonstrated by His kindness to us in Christ Jesus,"

Ephesians 2:6-7

BONUS BOOSTERS at the end of each chapter will explore and unveil the unfathomable magnificence of this scripture and how we can translate this eternal truth from pinnacle to practical.

IN CHRIST, BELIEVERS HAVE ALREADY BEEN RAISED UP AND SEATED IN HEAVENLY PLACES!

2

HOW TO OPEN UP TO LOVE AND STOP REJECTING ENCOURAGEMENT

If I am not for myself, who will be for me? If I am not for others, what am I? And if not now, when?

-Rabbi Hillel

The first step toward uplifted living involves an honest look inside your own heart. To what degree are you inwardly resistant to the good news of what Christ accomplished in and for you? Do you deflect personal encouragement? Have you been discouraged about starting or completing a particular project, ministry focus, or personal goal? Honestly, I surmise that we are all nodding our heads here. A good majority of the people I personally surveyed over the years on this issue admitted to some level of self-sabotaging, procrastination, and running on low when it came to knowing how to receive encouragement. We can be our own worst critics and totally miss out on the deluge of God's love and power available to us.

Here's a story from many years ago demonstrating to me that I had to take a look at my defenses and change my reactions to incoming encouragement to complete God-inspired assignments. It illustrates a common, even subconscious, resistance predicament and the solution. I'm guessing that you will relate.

"What in the world is holding you back, Honey?" My husband's kind, brown eyes caught mine for a moment; quickly, I looked away. I sipped my iced tea and gazed at the clear, blue lake just yards from our French café table.

"I really think you should write that book. You know how many people have loved your teaching series on raising kids for greatness. Nobody tells it as you do." These wonderful words of optimism struck my ears but ricocheted from my heart like gunshot off a bulletproof vest.

"I'm serious," he pursued with passion, "you've got a degree in Creative Writing, a wealth of practical experience, and great stories to tell. With so many parents feeling inadequate about their parenting skills, I know it could be a best-seller." I nodded my head and smiled appreciatively, but inside I wasn't buying it. He could tell. Trying another angle to penetrate my invisible fortress, he reached across the table and held my hand. "You know, with summer coming up, it would be a great time to just spend the afternoons writing. Don't you think?"

It didn't matter. My reluctance poisoned what should have been a magical, even romantic moment. Every loving sentence returned like a boomerang, disappearing into space.

"What is holding me back?" I asked myself. I longed to believe and absorb his sincere, uplifting words, but just couldn't. More discouraged than ever by the awareness of my closed heart, I abruptly changed the subject. I had to sort this out alone. Strolling around the lake that afternoon, I paused to stare at the mountain peaks' reflection in the still water. The spring-green slopes still capped with white were so majestic. Still troubled, I prayed, "What is going on with me? I can dish out encouragement to almost anyone, but receiving it is a completely different thing." A few steps later, an explanatory image flashed into my mind...of playing "airplane" many years ago with my little son.

Pureed sweet potatoes decorated his blonde hair and my kitchen floor, but none had penetrated his clamped little mouth. Strapped in his high chair with a smirk on his face, my determined two-year-old knew that the battle was on, and he was winning. Frustrated, I resorted to the airplane game.

"Rrrrrrrrreeeeeeee!" My tongue trilled and sputtered, trying to imitate a plane engine. The dripping spoon swirled in circle eights through the air. He giggled with glee, entertained by my antics.

"Look! He's coming in for a landing. Open wide!"

But the airplane hangar remained sealed tight and more orange goo exploded, this time landing all over my white silk shirt. That was it. The game was over and my toddler had triumphed...to his own detriment.

I threw a stone into the lake and laughed at my next thought.

"So, I get it, God; You are playing airplane with me through the words of my husband and I am the toddler, refusing exactly what I need, right?" I knew the answer. Shockingly, Almighty God through my husband was trying to feed and fortify me with nutritious inspiration, but I spat it right out on the floor. How rude. How ridiculous. But sometimes we are like that with incoming encouragement. We just won't open up. I had to find out why.

It's not the mountain we conquer, but ourselves. -Author Unknown

Recognizing my membership in the secret society of the "un-encouragable," one thing became obvious to me early on: the ability to receive boosting encouragement to live "UP" must begin inside of us—in the core of our being—in our hearts. Fascinating discoveries followed.

One thing became obvious to me early on: the ability to receive boosting encouragement to live "UP" must begin inside of us - in the core of our being - in our hearts.

Ground Zero: Our Hearts

A term coined by a good friend fits here: heart lids. Just as our eyelids automatically close to protect our eyes from harm, our hearts develop a kind of "lid." Negative judgments of ourselves combined with harsh criticisms inflicted upon us by others weld together to form a massive shield around our hearts. It clamps tightly, like armor, attempting to protect us from pain. These protective reactions can in some cases, be there for good reason. We should wisely guard our hearts against actual damaging abuse, but *not* from the Lord's genuine love and transformational encouragement.

Some of our heart-lids locked down like dungeon doors years ago. They shut out potential intruding evil villains, true, but also repel kind visitors bringing genuine inspiration and support. In a quest for safety, sometimes we end up isolated and insulated from the very force that would lift us and launch us into our life's full purpose. So how do we know the difference? How can we venture out of the dungeon of despair and find hope again? Can we dare open our rusty heart lids? The chapters of this book present much more than "self-help principles," but enlightening truths to help us soar to our highest with the help of the greatest Encourager of all.

Heart Transplant

My trajectory changed when my relationship with Jesus unveiled the exit to this trap. Ezekiel 36:26 promises a supernatural heart transplant available to us as we come to Him. "I will give you a new heart and put a new spirit in you; I will remove from you your heart of stone and give you a heart of flesh."

Proverbs 13:12 says it this way, "Hope deferred makes the heart sick, but a desire fulfilled is a tree of life." I have found that there is no safer place to open up and expose your life dents, your "sick heart" than before our compassionate Creator in the privacy of His chambers of unconditional love. My heart transplant and healing started with faith in Jesus Christ. His perfect love banished my vulnerability and fear. Being forgiven and cleansed from all shame and condemnation because of what *He did* for me on the cross brought genuine heart peace and security. This One with nail-scarred hands truly understands wounds and will tenderly examine, diagnose, and prescribe everything we need for our heart's healing. Healing fuels us to fulfill our life's design.

Please don't pull back and stop reading if you're not sure about that. Just know that a miraculous rendezvous is waiting for you. Jesus said, "Are you weary, carrying a heavy burden? Then come to Me. I will refresh your life, for I am your oasis. Simply join your life with mine. Learn my ways and you'll discover that I'm gentle, humble, and easy to please. You will find refreshment and rest in me. For all that I require of you will be pleasant and easy to bear." Matthew 11:28-30 (TPT) What an invitation.

Renewing the Soul

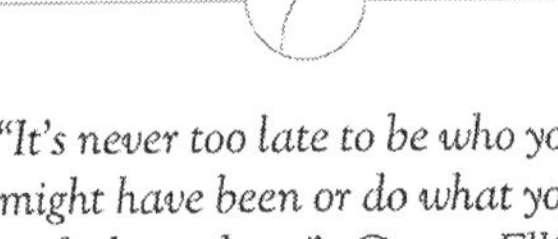

"It's never too late to be who you might have been or do what you might have done." -George Elliot

Healing starts in the heart or the spirit but continues into the renewing of our soul: our mind, emotions, and will. Advancing through future chapters, we'll explore just how to renew our minds. We will be liberated by tracking down and snuffing out old mental habits, residues of hurt, deprecating self-judgments, and the self-protective instincts that formed these shields that mutilate incoming strength. Identifying and erasing what I call negative "soul tattoos" will change our lives in vital ways. Gaining truth from the Supreme Encourager, Jesus Christ will launch us into a new view of ourselves, new strength to accomplish our dreams and enjoy a "UP lifestyle" we never thought possible. In that place of restoration, we can pick up and complete those divine assignments, personal goals, and purposeful projects. One of my favorite quotes is this: "It's never too late to be who you might have been or do what you might have done!" George Elliot: an extraordinary female writer who had to use a male alias to get published in her time.

As the apostle Paul prayed for the believers in Ephesus,

this is my sincere desire and prayer for you as you take this journey:

I pray that Christ will be more and more at home in your heart as you trust in him.

May your roots go down deep into the soil of God's marvelous love.

And may you have the power to understand, as all God's people should, how wide, how long, how high, and how deep His love really is.

May you experience the love of Christ, though it is so great you will never fully understand it. Then you will be filled with the fullness of life and power that comes from God. Ephesians 3:17-19 NLT

Here is the headwater where we uncap the river source of all encouragement and dive into pure pools of refreshment. As His love flows in, a surplus flows out. He reveals His faithfulness, and deeper security follows. He gives His heart totally to us, and we give ourselves unreservedly to Him. Christ gladly takes up the post of protecting our hearts. Our hinged, heart-lids creak open to let in fortifying comfort and joy that we thought would never return. Once we open up internally, then we successfully overcome the challenges that come externally. A gushing current of life rises in us and overflows to others...and that's where the real adventure begins.

Start by taking the Personal Assessment Questionnaire to locate your starting place. And why not invite a friend or two to join in the journey? I believe it's much more fun to grow with others. Really, what is there to lose? Only fear, depression, and mediocrity.

BONUS BOOSTER

"And God raised us up with Christ and seated us with Him in the heavenly realms in Christ Jesus, in order that in the coming ages He might display the surpassing riches of His grace, demonstrated by His kindness to us in Christ Jesus," Ephesians 2:6-7

This awe-inspiring scripture is under-preached and tremendously under-believed. And yet it is a sovereign and significant event that has already happened to every person who has put their faith in Christ. Paul, writing to the church in Ephesus, includes a powerful prayer for them (and us) to have a *supernatural revelation* about what he presents, knowing that without it, they would choke on the incredible content.

For this reason, ever since I heard about your faith in the Lord Jesus and your love for all the saints, I have not stopped giving thanks for you, remembering you in my prayers, that the God of our Lord Jesus Christ, the glorious Father, may give you a spirit of wisdom and revelation in your knowledge of Him. I ask that the eyes of your heart may be enlightened, so that you may know the hope of His calling, the riches of His glorious inheritance in the saints, and the surpassing greatness of His power to us who believe. These are in accordance with the working of His mighty strength, which He exerted in Christ when He raised Him from the dead and seated Him at His right hand in the heavenly realms, far above all rule and authority, power and dominion, and every name that is named, not only in the present age but also in the one to come. Ephesians 1:17-21 Pray it for yourself and your loved ones.

PERSONAL ASSESSMENT QUESTIONNAIRE

It's always good to locate and assess where you are right now. How encouraged and/or "encouragable" are you? Be brutally honest with yourself as you take this quick survey. Choose the response that is most true of you for each statement.

A. Receiving Compliments

1. When someone gives me an encouraging compliment, my first reaction is...

- I usually receive it fully, and say "Thank you"
- Half of the time I appear to receive it, but INSIDE I doubt and downplay it
- I often reject it.

Comments?________________________________

2. When you do reject incoming compliments, analyze how you usually do it.

- By discrediting the person giving it (He/she wants something or is just trying to make me feel good)
- By discrediting yourself
- Other:________________________________

Comments?________________________________

B. Encouragement Level

3. Which statement most accurately describes you?

- The majority of the time I am encouraged and "up"
- About half the time I am encouraged and "up"
- I am discouraged and negative most of the time

Comments?________________________________

C. Size of your circle of encouragers

4. How large is your circle of encouragers?

- I have several people in my life that I could turn to for true encouragement
- I have at least one good friend I can turn to for encouragement
- I often have no one I feel comfortable turning to for encouragement

Comments?________________________________

D. Encouraging Yourself Skill

5. When no one is around to encourage you, which statement best describes how you deal with discouragement?

- It is natural for me to strengthen and encourage myself most of the time
- It is challenging to encourage myself, but sometimes I succeed
- It feels unnatural to encourage myself and I rarely do

Comments?________________________________

E. Receive Encouragement from God

6. How much tangible/relevant encouragement do you get from your relationship with God? (Remember, He already knows and won't be mad if you are honest.)

- Most days I receive encouragement
- Occasionally I receive encouragement
- Rarely I receive encouragement
- None, because I really don't have a relationship yet

Comments?________________________________

F. Freedom to Ask for Help

7. When you need encouragement, how freely do you ask for it?

- I am usually quick and bold to ask for

encouragement

- I am often reluctant to show or share that I need encouragement
- Only if someone inquires directly do I ask for help

G. Transparency

8. How many people are close enough to you and know what you're going through that give you encouragement?

- none
- one person
- about three people
- more than three

Comments?________________________________

H. Outflow of Encouragement

9. How encouraging are you to others?

- I express encouragement easily and often
- I express encouragement on special occasions
- I find it difficult to express encouragement

Comments?________________________________

I. Taking Courage in Difficult Times

10. How easily do you yield to discouragement?

- I melt pretty easily
- I yield to discouragement about half the time
- I am fairly quick to stand up against it
- I aggressively resist it

J. Encouragement toward more specific goals, projects, divine assignments:

11. Retake questions 3 – 10 with a different color pencil/pen directed at these. Use the comment line if needed.

Small-Group Discussion – Journal Reflections

ONE: OPEN UP YOUR HEART

Answer with a friend, a group, or individually in a journal.

1. Examine your survey results and talk about your responses to each question.

2. In which of the areas of encouragement below do you feel strongest and the weakest? Why?

Response to encouraging compliments

Your present level of encouragement

Circle of encouragement

Self-encouragement skill

Ease at receiving encouragement from God

Ease at receiving encouragement from others

The practice of encouraging others

Resistance to discouragement

3. Define "heart lids." Do you relate?

4. When you answered questions 3-10 with regard to your goals, projects, or divine assignments, what did you learn?

Are there unfulfilled goals and divine assignments you have given up on or have on the shelf?

Prayer and Journaling Suggestions:

Use the Ephesians 3:17-19 prayer contained in this chapter and spend some time praying individually or for one another in pairs for open hearts and a fresh revelation of God's love. Journal your thoughts, feelings, and questions about your survey results or anything triggered by this chapter.

3

HOW TO CLEAN UP NEGATIVE SOUL TATTOOS

Tracing and Erasing Soul Tattoos

The soul is dyed the color of its thoughts.
-Heraclitus

The next hurdle is to identify and remove false notions and black labels contrary to the Word and opinion of God that weigh us down. I'll share how even after coming to know Christ, I discovered a sinister, soul tattoo that had been dragging me under for decades. It was exposed and then powerfully destroyed, setting me free into a whole new dimension of joy and liberty. Perhaps one of your hidden soul tattoos will come into the light for eradication. You'll never get to the peak of your destination carrying extra backpacks full of rocks and steel. Let's roll those down the hill of new revelation. I trust my transparent stories will help.

"Your sister just gave birth to twin boys!" dad announced, elated. "Jump in the car, Claudia Jean, and let's go to the sports department of JC Penney, right now."

"Daddy, I've never seen you break the speed limit before."

"Do as I say and not as I do, Claudia Jean. We've got to get my boys some equipment!"

"At one hour old?" I wondered. His excitement had a strange effect on me at seventeen years old. Why I suddenly became quiet and reserved, I didn't know.

Inside, he grabbed two, red baseball hats, two plastic bats, two balls, two gloves, and two footballs, piling what he couldn't carry into my arms. Rudely impatient with the clerk who was not checking us out fast enough, he paid cash and rushed out the store doors, carrying enough sports supplies for the twins' lifetime.

Trailing behind him, I wondered, "Why does this make

me uncomfortably sad? I'm glad to be an aunt, I'm happy for my sister..." I dismissed my feelings as crazy. Wildly speeding to the hospital, we parked crookedly and I ran behind him from the parking lot into the hospital to greet my new nephews. It would be years before I understood my mixed emotions.

Unsolved Mysteries: Tracing A Tattoo

Most of us have shadow-like, soul tattoos from our past. They lurk just beneath our skin. These black insignias try to define us. Like question marks in our souls, they leave us doubting our personal worth on a subconscious level. They haunt us by night and keep us feeling insecure by day. We've lived with them for so long that they almost seem second nature, even normal. To access and live in encouragement and joy, we must expose these black scars and let them be supernaturally erased.

Soul tattoos are false edicts declaring things like, "You are flawed," "You don't matter," "You are unworthy," "You are unwanted," "You are stupid," "You are a bother," "You can't do this," "You don't belong," or "God doesn't love you," ...fill in the blank. Inscribed in my thinking early in my life was a subconscious taunt, "You can never, ever measure up." This invisible measuring stick followed me around browbeating me continually, "No matter what you accomplish, you will always fall short." Fall short of what?

That's what I had to find out. My first clue: a restless striving. One effective way to hunt down a negative tattoo is to recognize an area where you are striving to overcompensate. I strove tirelessly in school to get straight A's, become the head cheerleader and a strong softball player. Nevertheless, I noted that the thrill of each and every successful achievement faded quickly like sidewalk chalk in the rain.

This tattoo would spoil every victory with, "Claudia, that's really nothing, you're not as good as so-and-so." Cringing at these decrees, but determined to feel significant, I would raise the high bar toward the next hurdle of performance. Do you relate? Examine your own inner dialogue. I continued this inane cycle of "successful defeat" like a caged hamster tenaciously running on his silver wheel *all night long*, pathetically ending up in the exact same spot the next morning. All the glowing report cards, awards, and blue ribbons in the world could never scrub off this devilish false belief.

This ruthless pattern of achievement and dissatisfaction intensified even as I pursued spiritual endeavors. As a new Christian in my college years, this time I labored leading Bible studies, sharing my faith, joining overseas missions trips, and doing everything with 500% zeal. But I was nagged by the impression that there was always *more* I should or could have done...this time for Jesus. Robbed of genuine joy in the journey, and tormented with the lie that I could never measure up with Him either, all the emphasis was the obsession to climb the next spiritual mountain...only to find that familiar discontentment at the top.

Coach Jesus to the Rescue

I have seen how the kind Spirit of God orchestrates just the right time for healing in our souls. He will gingerly uncover an infected wound inside, pain that we'd rather not look at, in order to drive us into His arms of love. He's not being cruel bringing these aches to the surface. Like a boil that has to be lanced, He's setting us up for supernatural healing and deliverance. Desperate for release from this phantom stalking me, I finally ran into those arms of refuge for help. The answer I sought surfaced from deep within while communing with Him. A gentle inner voice said, "It's all about you and your dad..."

My dad...a timekeeper for the UCLA Bruins basketball team in the days of champion Lou Alcindor, introduced me to this giant star. Looking up in awe from my young, three-foot vantage point, about as tall as Lou's knees, I could barely see up to his face. That's how my dad always seemed to me...larger than life.

At eleven years old, I was his proud, pony-tailed "batgirl" when he coached our local boys' Little League baseball team. Dressed in his team's tee-shirt, a blue baseball cap, and boy's Levis rolled up at the bottom like the guys, I fetched all the bats they threw as if it was the most important task on the planet.

Reflecting on this, it suddenly hit me why I so often felt like a failure, why I could *never* measure up. All my life, I had subconsciously tried to do what I thought would *most* please this hero of mine. I adored him. He adored sports. I recalled a vague memory of how he talked about wanting a boy before my youngest sister was born. Distorted impressions in my mind created the *perfect* set-up for imagining myself to be an ongoing disappointment. As the middle of three daughters, I could never be the one thing I concluded he wanted most. I could *never* be a ...a son.

So that's it! I wept with relief the moment this dramatic revelation dawned. No wonder I felt those misgivings about his joy at the birth of his grandsons. It was just another confirmation that I fell short. It seemed *so* obvious now. Truth sets you free.

While closing my eyes to thank God for showing me the origin of this festering tattoo, a full-color, three-dimensional, movie clip flashed before my mind's eye. A familiar, fully-lit football field appeared. I could almost smell the freshly cut grass. I remembered standing hundreds of times on the sidelines under the field lights in my maroon and white sweater and plaid pleated skirt leading thousands of fans in cheers for the Claremont High Wolfpack. In those days, the closest a girl could get to being a star football player was to become the head cheerleader for the team. Crystal clear now, I saw how deep inside, part of my motivation for cheering was to gain the craved attention and approval of the superman of my life: my father.

But this scene was different. Only Jesus and I were standing there. We stood together on the expansive field at about the 20-yard line. Under the bright lights, He held a football and tilted His head while eyeing the goal. He passed me a quick, knowing smile, and then turned to execute the kick. The ball propelled perfectly upward and at the precise moment it crossed the goal post, Jesus turned to me, laughing and pointing His finger right at my nose, and shouted, "Hey, Claudia! *You score with Me!*"

Euphoric energy surged through me as His words shattered my false notions about myself into a million pieces. The incessant search for approval was over. "You score with Me!" branded a new logo in the depths of my heart, a tattoo of truth autographed by God Himself.

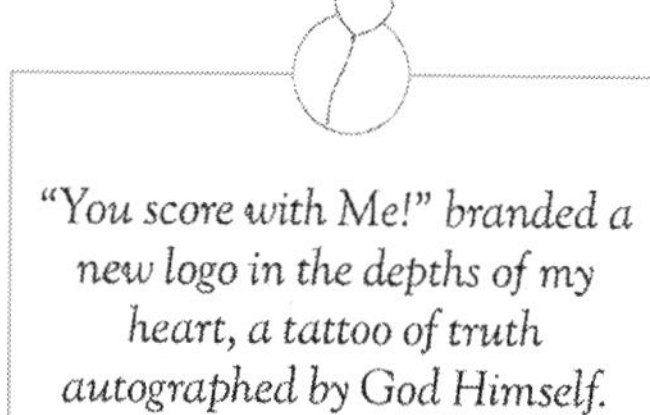

Jesus used the poignant, football-field imagery, a scene of my impossible quest for significance, to forever settle the gnawing issue. My lifelong quest to please my father was buried there on the football field that night. The epitaph could have read, "Here lie the final remains of Claudia Bausman Porter's aching pursuit of approbation. She scores with her Creator and that's all that matters."

In His eyes, I found favor *apart* from straight A's or a sports medal. His four words, "You score with Me," broke the abusive measuring stick into a trillion splinters. Laughter turned into irrepressible shouts of joy. I had every reason to rejoice. The King of kings and the Lord of lords favored me *just because*. I scored with my eternal heavenly Father. The coach of heaven chose and loved me, not for any achievement, but just for who I am to Him. My union with Him gave me a totally new identity based on His work on the cross and a right standing now with Him as a free gift.

That encounter so many years ago popped a cork of celebration in my life. Caverns of depression were cleared out and filled with fresh hope. Once a soul tattoo is exposed and Jesus inscribes His words, His opinion of you in its place, a party in your soul breaks out. It's almost as if

He installs a sparkling water dispenser inside you. You can tap into it at any time. The effervescence of His presence gives new carbonation to every dimension of your life. As long as you drink from this supply, the party inside never ends.

Other tattoo brands: Nicknames

"Bird Legs," "Bookworm," "Lazy Bones," "Weirdo," "Fatso," "Dunce," "Retarded," "Cry Baby," "Noodle Brain," "Space Cadet," "Loser," "Bo Ugly," "Small Fry, and the list of curses goes on and on. The naked truth is that often negative nicknames leave scars. This was the case for a girl we will call Julie.

The Girl Scout camp cabin near the lake had a cold draft. All the sixth-grade girls nestled in their sleeping bags close together...except for one. Claire rolled over to get comfortable and noticed a little flash of light in the corner. A strong chemical smell assaulted her nose.

"Julie, is that you?"

"Yeah."

Pulling herself up onto her elbows to look at her glow-in-the-dark watch, Claire whispered loudly, "It's only four o'clock in the morning. What are you doing awake over there?"

"Oh, nothing...I couldn't sleep. Go back to sleep. I'm sorry I woke you up."

"But what is that smell, Julie?"

Claire crawled over to see for herself what Julie was hiding under her sleeping bag.

"Nail polish? You're putting on nail polish for outdoor camp? Come on! We'll be hiking, swimming, climbing trees, and making campfires. Why would you even care about your nails?"

But Julie got up every morning at 4 am to paint her nails; they just had to match her outfit for the day. From adolescence onward, she followed this ritual of spending two hours every morning making sure her clothes and make-up were perfect. She wouldn't go out in public without a magazine cover look, perfectly painted nails, matching shoes, and accessories for each outfit. This obsession with her physical appearance continued far into her adult years. She entered beauty contest after beauty contest to prove...to prove what? She didn't know.

Julie forgot all about the childhood nickname she was running from, until one night when she sitting in the front row at a prayer service. She was reapplying her Dusty Rose lipstick just as Mary, the pastor's wife, leaned over to whisper something in her ear.

"What did you say?" Julie inquired with a look of amazement.

"I said, 'As we were just praying here, I had an impression from the Lord saying that if you ask Him, He will give you a new name.'"

"A new name? Why would I want a new name," she pondered. Looking a bit puzzled, she responded anyway.

"Okay," cautiously she prayed, "Lord, what is the new name you want to give me?" and then bowed her head to listen. Clearly, these words passed through her mind, "You are beautiful to Me."

"Beautiful? Me? Beautiful to You?"

"No, I'm Bo Ugly." Bo Ugly. She had done everything possible to forget and abolish that childhood nickname, but once again it stared her in the face. Her family resented her for the difficult pregnancy her mother endured while carrying her. Older and unprepared to have another child, her mother had gone deaf and had life-threatening complications during her pregnancy with Julie.

Branded as a nuisance before she was even born, Julie became the scapegoat. Bo Ugly seemed the fitting nickname. Later, when the pain of that horrible pregnancy had passed, Julie eventually won the affection of her family, but the nickname stuck. Like a rusty, heavy anchor attached to her "ship," an all-penetrating sense of shame held her down and kept her from sailing freely in life. A part of her always had to hide.

She struggled in vain for years to escape this old tattoo that dyed her self-image "ugly." But in this sovereign moment, the noose that had strangled her like an umbilical cord around her neck was about to be cut off. The Spirit of God took the divine shears of God's word to sever it. He then inscribed a new inscription upon her heart: "Beautiful to the Lord." This new name came with a confirming scripture: "You are altogether beautiful, my darling, and there is no blemish in you," Song of Solomon 4:7. Tears and Lancôme black mascara streamed down her cheeks as she accepted this amazing new brand. God's word re-colored her from ugly to beautiful.

Julie told me that she could never feel ugly again because, "When the Lord re-names you, every other name, curse, and negative word fades away."

A side note for parents, coaches, teachers, siblings, and everyone who influences a child. Beware. Our words contain the power of life and death, especially when spoken about children who look up to us. They don't have filters to balance or interpret our words. They often just believe them. We have the awesome power to curse them with a negative soul tattoo or bless them. Practical lessons on blessing them are ahead.

Live your imagination, not your history.
-Stephen Covey

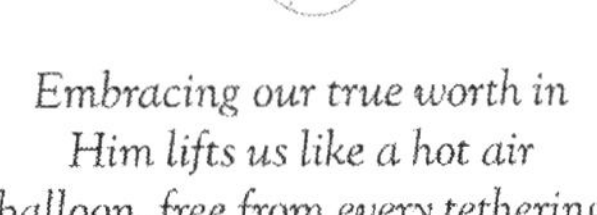

Embracing our true worth in Him lifts us like a hot air balloon, free from every tethering weight and rope.

Not all such internal impressions originate from careless or abusive external influences. These shackling scars can also be self-inflicted, developed by our receiving and believing a lie even in a generally happy family situation as in my case. Whether from childhood nicknames or other painful experiences that influenced our views of ourselves, we can release ourselves from the handcuffs of hidden tattoos. We can tear down strongholds of the mind that have formed false definitions of ourselves by receiving the eternal truth of our settled identity in Christ.

No matter the source, when God's powerful, eternal word breaks in to unchain us from these fictitious, inner fetters; we are thrust into a liberating realm of incredible exhilaration on the inside. Embracing our true worth in Him lifts us like a hot air balloon, free of every tethering weight and rope. Truth sets us free and lifts us above the negative pull of this earth into the encouragement zone, a zone far above earthly limitations where all things are possible...where we can live UP no matter what we have endured in the past. We can soar to tremendous heights and uncharted territory with Christ.

Take His hand and let Him trace and erase the soul tattoos under your skin. Silence that inner critical voice. Let go of your history and start experiencing a new dimension of hope. Be who you really are now in Christ.

Think Up to Stay Up

Maintaining this new altitude will require that we learn to direct our mind traffic. Staying free in a lifestyle of optimism requires learning the follow-up practice of taking control of our thought life. We have the power to direct the traffic that goes through our minds. The battle for our continued well-being always starts and ends right here in the mind. Living UP entails thinking UP. So, if we had a daily printout of your thoughts, how would it read?

Here's a critical fact. Every deception and downward detour comes *first* as a thought, as a suggestion. When I am aware of feeling a bit downcast, I stop and look at what negative lies have been trying to nest in my head. Once identified, I reject those joy predators by affirming what is true as revealed in the Word of God. It is *amazing* how our mood can change by switching our focus to meditating on the truth of His promise, His analysis, which is the exact opposite of where our thoughts were going.

This is the *true essence of spiritual warfare.* Even Jesus was tempted with lies about his identity and mission, but He did not believe and act on those lies. "For we do not have a high priest who is unable to sympathize with our weaknesses, but we have one who has been tempted in every way, just as we are–yet was without sin," Hebrews 4:1. This verse clearly separates a temptation introduced into the mind from sin. What great news! I used to feel polluted and so guilty when evil thoughts traveled through my mind. Then I realized that having the thought alone was not evil, but *acting upon it* would be. What a relief it is to know this fact. We have the power to reject and resist thoughts. They are like vultures circling overhead, seeking somewhere to nest and peck. Our job is to *not* let them nest.

Jesus was tempted in the same way we are, in the thought realm. He was tempted but He never yielded to the bait. Demonic temptation always begins with the introduction of thoughts contrary to the Word of God, as is demonstrated in the gospel of Matthew chapter four, verses three and four.

"And the tempter came and said to Him, "If You are the Son of God, command that these stones become bread." Jesus countered with, "It is written, man shall not live on bread alone, but on every word that proceeds from the mouth of God." Jesus rejected the thought that He had to prove He was the Son of God and instead, spoke the truth of the scripture, thus extinguishing the fiery dart of Satan designed to get Him off track.

The enemy of our soul was defeated at the cross. He has *no* power except the power of lies. He traffics in deception. Jesus called him "the father of lies." It's only when we accept, believe, and act upon those falsehoods that our adversary finds inroads into our lives to pull us down and under. Effective spiritual warfare involves firmly and continually "directing" the traffic passing through our minds. Paul admonishes us strongly about this vital tactic in 2 Corinthians 10:5. "We demolish arguments and every pretension that sets itself up against the knowledge of God, and we *take captive every thought* to make it obedient to Christ."

How we respond to dark thoughts about our worth, identity, or actions makes *all* the difference. All three times that Jesus was tempted in this passage, He responded by quoting the scripture, "It is written." That's exactly what we can do. Instead of believing and acting on a deceptive thought like, "You are worthless," "You are warped," "Steal that sweater," "Have an affair with that person,"... fill in the blank, we can *resist* the temptation-thought and replace it with a scriptural "It is written." In speaking the Word of God, we cast down and *send away* the marauding lies that come to devour us, and our enemy has to flee. As believers, we depend on His power inside to remind us to meditate on *His* words and perspective. This cuts through fog and falsehoods and defines what's real.

We can't be passive in this battle in our minds if we are determined to live UP. We should have the same reaction to lies attacking our minds as we would if we heard the sounds of an armed and dangerous thief trying to break into our home. We wouldn't be nonchalant and open the door to welcome him. We would rise up, set off security alarms, call 911, and defend ourselves. So when the arch-bandit of our soul introduces ideas sent to rob us of our confidence and joy or to get us off course, *how much more* should we aggressively resist and stand in the armor of God. We should assert verbally, as Jesus did, the truths written in scripture that counteract the lie being presented. The spoken word of God, called the sword of the Spirit, will pulverize the poisonous lies.

We must consciously arrest old thought patterns and actively take those thoughts captive. If we don't, they will affect our emotions and lead to making poor choices, and we will land right back into depression or fear...slain merely by unchecked thoughts!

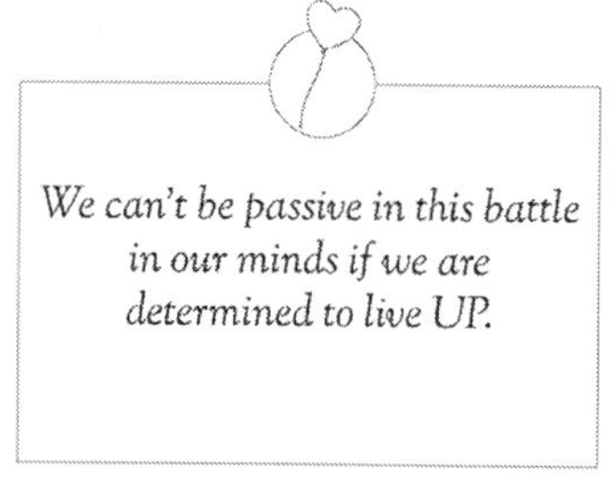

Philemon 1:6 contains a powerful truth to apply every day against the barrage of falsehoods that plague our minds. "And I pray that the fellowship of your faith may become effective through the knowledge of *every good thing which is in you* for Christ's sake." We can start *acknowledging* the reality of all the good things that are in us *now* because Christ is in us. It will *completely* change our focus and silence the static.

God's powerful Word destroys *every* stronghold built up in our heads. Truth dispels them. Had I understood His unconditional love for me as a young girl, I would have not been susceptible to the deceit that brought such agony for *so* many years.

New meditations lead to new emotions, new emotions to new actions which lead to new habits and a new lifestyle altogether. Today, we can begin to think UP, feel UP, and live UP. Activating a spiritual lie detector over our minds sets and keeps us free. Fling that back-pack of fictional identity off the cliff and resume life with fresh energy, free of every foul soul scar. Grasp how the Creator views us every day and experience a new level of living UP, tattoo-free!

BONUS BOOSTER

Christ was not only raised from the dead but after His ascension was then *seated in heavenly places at the right hand of God* as the coronated King of Kings and Lord of Lords. We hear this part preached about and "get it." But the *Ephesians 2:6-7 verses* reveal that in Him *we were also raised and seated there* with Him and it boggles our minds. Until we see that we were united with Him on the cross, in His death, burial, and resurrection, and His seating in heavenly places, we haven't comprehended the fullness of our salvation.

Everything that happened to Jesus on the cross, in the grave, in His resurrection, and His seating in power,

HAPPENED TO ALL BELIEVERS, TOO!

Small-Group Discussion – Journal Reflections

TWO: CLEAN UP ANY SOUL TATTOOS

Answer with a friend, a group, or individually in a journal.

1. What were your nicknames?

2. Did you view any nicknames as negative?

3. How did negative ones affect you?

4. Have you ever struggled with the feeling you just didn't measure up? Explain.

5. Can you trace back to where you got that message or another negative tattoo?

6. Do you often feel like you have to perform to be loved?

7. What other labels have been like soul tattoos to your journey?

8. What does God's word say about you in contrast to the tattoos?

9. Read these scriptural truths about you about your new identity out loud.

10. Read over these most astonishing statements made about and for you.

(Paraphrased...check out the sources!)

I, your Father, love you as much as I love Jesus! (John 17:23)

You were worth the blood of My Son. (1 Peter 1:18-19)

I have made everything right between you and Me. (Romans 5:1)

When I look at you now, I see Jesus. (Ephesians 4:24, 2 Corinthians 5:17 & 21)

I will never betray or leave you. (Hebrews 13:5)

These things that I do, you shall do and even greater. (John 14:12)

Live intimately dependent on Me and I will live in You and whatever you ask the Father in My name shall be given to you. (John 15:7)

Nothing shall separate you from my love. (Romans 8:38-39)

My grace is more than enough for you. (2 Corinthians 12:9)

No matter what temptation you face, I will show a way to escape. (Hebrews 10:13)

My loving-kindness never ends. My compassion toward you is new every morning.

I will always be faithful to you! (Lamentations 3:23-24)

No matter what pain or hardship you face, I will turn it around for your good.

(Romans 8:28)

I have amazing plans for you, to give you a future and a hope. (Jeremiah 29:11)

Pray for one another to receive erased tattoos and a new view of themselves.

4

HOW TO HOOK UP TO THE GREATEST ENCOURAGER OF ALL TIME

The Spirit of God

It is for your good that I am going away.
Unless I go away, the Encourager will not come to you;
but if I go, I will send Him to you.
-Jesus Christ: John 16:7

Liberation from our past wounds and those limiting

paradigms is truly glorious. Opening up to a God-inspired view of ourselves and embracing His love and call on our lives is a wild and adventurous ride. No longer ignorant of the schemes to pull us down, and clearer about Christ's opinion of us, we can begin living in a new dimension (seated in heavenly places next to the Father) enjoying His gift of perfect, right standing with Him. Now that we know what to do when "vultures" try to nest in our brains, *we are ready to venture ahead.*

This chapter is vitally important to enable us to endure the suffering we will inevitably face living on this fallen planet. How can we live UP when regular disappointment and pain come crashing into our lives? Loss of loved ones, personal failures, betrayal, sickness, financial setbacks, broken relationships, tragedies of every size and shape will at some point trespass upon our pathway. Can we find a sustainable, sturdy source of heart strength and consolation in these times of raw suffering? Thankfully, yes. And the kind of courage we can experience is not flimsy, paper-thin, superficial, or mustered up in our own strength. Hallelujah. Jesus told His disciples of an unimaginable provision: the third person of the eternal Trinity, who would be sent to comfort, strengthen them for service, and refill them (and us) in times of dizzying trouble.

Jesus wasn't joking. Near the end of His earthly mission,

He told His disciples that He was leaving them and that *that* was going to be even *better* for them. I can imagine Peter now, blurting out, "Oh, right, Lord! How could *anything* be better than having You with us? You heal the lepers, raise people from the dead, pay those rotten Roman taxes with coins from the mouth of a fish, and tell off the religious hypocrites. Maybe John interrupted with, "But more than that, Lord, You truly love us. You love us as we've never been loved before." Looking at the ground, perhaps Peter finished with, "Even...even when we fail so miserably. How could anything be better than that?"

Jesus probably knowingly grinned as He went on to prepare them for the soon coming gift: the third Person of the Trinity. He had shown them the works and heart of the Father, lived before them as the Son, and now whets their spiritual appetite for encountering God, the Holy Spirit. What does this have to do with living up in a down world? Everything.

"Unless I go away, the Encourager will not come to you; but if I go, I will send Him to you," John 16:7. He had their full attention. They don't want Him to leave but are intrigued by His words of promise. "So who's this Encourager?" I can almost hear them ask. Jesus sketches a portrait of this identical-in-heart member of the Godhead, using titles like Counselor, Comforter, and Encourager. Yes, one of God's self-given names is Encourager. That's a new concept for many of us. Encourager in Greek is the word "Paraclete," which means "one called alongside to help." Strength was on the way. I bet the disciples were listening intently now to these attractive and unconventional descriptions.

"To inspire" means "to exhilarate, to cheer, to gladden, and imbue with inspiring ideas." How stunning it is to realize that this is what the Holy Spirit came to do for us every day.

Jesus continued explaining in John chapters fourteen through sixteen that He was about to leave them to fulfill the very reason for His coming. As the Lamb of God, within hours, He would offer Himself up to death on the cross for their sin and the sin of the whole world. He would triumphantly rise from the dead three days later and after His ascension, take His honored place at the right hand of the Father in heaven. As a result of His death and resurrection, He would soon inaugurate a new and better covenant based on better promises. He *had* to leave them to accomplish this. He promised not to leave them as orphans but to send this Encourager, this gift of the Holy Spirit who would guide, strengthen and reveal to them the meaning of His words. And they would *need* this gift, as they were definitely headed for some very rough waters.

Hooking Up to Heaven

Fully connecting to this heavenly inflow of support is imperative. Have you ever tried to water your flowers or lawn with hardly any water coming out of the hose? I have, and the problem was never the water source but the hose's connection to it. Either the nozzle end was not screwed on straight or tight enough allowing water to spew all over the faucet area, or the hose was twisted and bent, restricting the water flow. Getting to know God the Holy Spirit, and fully connecting to Him is indispensable to receiving the water-flow of unfailing encouragement in our lives.

Jesus was excited about this new hook-up that would be available to his disciples. His magnificent company would no longer be limited to one geographical location on earth where He physically walked with a few disciples. The miraculous, new-covenant arrangement would release His presence to live inside His followers *everywhere*. He would be able to indwell His body all over the earth, giving each believer constant access to God Almighty via the Person of the Holy Spirit. What a miraculous privilege. Now, in this new covenant that He was inaugurating, each believer would be enabled to connect the "hose" of his life to the Godhead and be filled to overflowing with the fullness of His being.

The divine third person of the Trinity would not just be *with* disciples as before the sending of the Holy Spirit, but would now supernaturally dwell *in* them! Living inside people...not in temples made of stone is what He's always wanted. "For we are the temple of the living God. As God said: 'I will live in them and walk among them. I will be their God, and they will be my people,'" 2 Corinthians 6:16. Our Creator, the One who created heaven and earth eternally longed to give us this sweet companionship and constant liaison with Him. Christianity is so far above being a "religion" but is at the core, a relationship. This life example brought the reality of "hooking up to God for relief" home to us when our daughter had just had back surgery.

Intravenous Help

"Honey, are you in severe pain?"

Fresh out of surgery from a dance injury, my teen daughter, nodded slightly, trying not to create more pain. I remembered the nurse's instructions. "See this button connected to her I.V.? When she wakes up and needs a painkiller, just push it. It will give her instant medication, just the amount she can safely have." So comforted by this marvelous provision for my beloved daughter, I firmly pushed the magic button for her relief. All moms and dads know that seeing their children in pain is worse than being in pain themselves. Naomi quickly fell into a deep, comfortable sleep, while I sat praying quietly. We praised

God often for this instant help button to get her through those first intense hours after surgery.

This illustrates in a small way, the magnificent operation of the Holy Spirit in our lives. Our heavenly Father has created a "pain-relief" system for you, too. As His child, you are interfaced with His presence through the Holy Spirit. He is ready at any moment, to dispense to you the exact measure of comfort, truth, and bolstering you need for every situation you face in your life. He *is* that comfort! Psalm 46:1 announces, "God is our refuge and our strength, an ever-present help in times of trouble." You "push the button" by simply calling on Him, acknowledging His presence and power at any time. You can come freely and boldly to this Great Physician, the Healer of your entire spirit, soul, and body.

Don't misunderstand, heartbreak and the melancholy that can accompany it often do not have an instant fix and God is not a drug. However, our daily relationship with Him provides a constant flow of hope and wisdom. He is always with us, understands our weaknesses, and is weaving an elegant tapestry of benefits even from the afflictions we navigate in this fallen world. "And we know that in all things God works for the good of those who love Him, who have been called according to His purpose," Romans 8:28.

Don't Live Unplugged

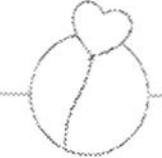

We have become His dwelling place, His living room, His home-sweet-home. This is the unfathomable destiny of every believer.

Our hairdryer, curling iron, refrigerator, computer, and all other electric appliances won't work if they are not plugged into a power source. We can yell at them to work or just simply plug them in for the results we want. In the same way, life on earth is flatly impotent without plugging ourselves intimately into His life in us. But living in union with Him, attached to His unfathomable wisdom, is far better than finding a treasure chest of gold.

The internet and the World Wide Web have made a *universe* of network-accessible information available. Never before have we had such instant access to this extensive embodiment of human knowledge. All we have to do is connect to it. In a similar way, fellowship with the Holy Spirit is our access to our Omnipotent, All-Knowing, Everlasting God.

"Things which eye has not seen and ear have not heard, and which have not entered the heart of man, all that God has prepared for those who love Him, For to us God *revealed them through the Spirit*; for the Spirit searches all things, even the depths of God. For who among men knows the thoughts of a man except for the spirit of the man, which is in him? Even so, the thoughts of God no one knows except the Spirit of God. Now we have received, not the spirit of the world, but the Spirit who is from God, that we might *know the things freely given* to us by God," 1 Corinthians 2:9-12.

When we receive Christ and the gift of God, the Holy Spirit, we connect to the vast, eternal resources of the Creator of the entire universe. This is astounding to contemplate. No matter what problem, perplexity, or adversity we face that distresses and disheartens, we can take possession of His uplifting power eternally now available to us. We can live in intimate fusion with Him and encounter His counsel continually. His Words will supply the precise lift and courage we need. God has, and we have access.

Where do we lack insight or fortitude? Investing in our relationship with Him and pursuing heartfelt fellowship brings the answer. As we spend time reading from His love letter, the Bible, a verse of scripture will "light up" as He "downloads" the insight or direction that we need. Even if we don't receive instant clarity, we will receive the peace and assurance of His presence and know the wisdom or provision is on the way.

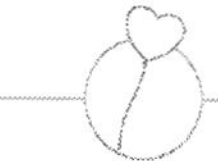

What can compare to this privilege of communing with the One who created all things, whose words echo throughout eternity and never return void? This is how you can face every challenge, connected with Deity!

Hearing Hints

But how do we know we are hearing from Him? A friend gave this analogy on the process of seeking to hear God's communication. Living in the Rocky Mountains, we revel in the stillness and quiet our woods and meadows afford. When I go outside, at first I am struck by the silence. I bask in the peace and solitude. Then my ears notice the increasing volume of different kinds of birds singing. Their combined surround-sound songs resonate loudly. What happens to make the sound change from silence to a full-scale bird concert? Although the bird songs previously filled the air all around me, my ear wasn't "tuned in" to hear their melodies. Then, in listening and reflection, I could pick up a whole new frequency of the sound being transmitted.

So it is with hearing from the Holy Spirit who is symbolized in the Bible as a dove. Often the jangling of anxious thoughts fills our minds. God calls but gets a busy signal. The noisy distractions of life and constant mind traffic drown out His "still small voice." When we step away from the clamor, and consciously "tune in" to heaven's transmissions, we begin to hear His subtle impressions. Increased time communing with Him in intimate friendship and meditating on His word automatically turn up the volume of His voice. When you spend time getting to know a friend, it becomes easy to recognize his or her voice.

Rarely does He speak audibly to our outer ears, but is often communicating with us on the inside. I have noticed that answers come to me just as I am waking from sleep in the morning. Impressions will surface exactly relevant to and in response to my prayer for wisdom. Remember, anything He impresses upon our hearts will always line up with what the scriptures teach. Discard any thoughts or impressions in contradiction with His word. He never gives guidance that violates it. He is so very faithful to give us the wisdom we need for every situation.

Clear Your Calendar

There is nothing better than
the encouragement of a good friend.
-Katherine Butler Hathaway

Have you ever had someone you really admired take an interest in spending time with you? A gracious and esteemed colleague once wanted to meet me for coffee. Flattered, astonished, and overjoyed, I cleared my calendar to meet with her. I couldn't wait to ask her questions about writing, gain from her wisdom, and unwrap the beauty I could see in her life. To meet face to face with someone you've admired from a distance is thrilling.

Imagine this: the God of heaven and earth has sent word that He wants us to meet with Him. From His palace in heaven, He has invited us to come and personally dine with Him. We cautiously enter the dining room to find a table arrayed with fine linen, elegant china, fragrant candles, and fresh flowers. An embossed place card engraved with our name in gold signifies that truly, this is our place at the table. There are only two place settings, yours and His. Already seated, He eagerly awaits our presence. We have His full attention. The only agenda for conversation is whatever is in our heart and whatever we want to know about His.

Get a glimpse of the honor bestowed by the Father. His ardent desire is to have a personal and close relationship with us. This is the mystery and majesty of Christianity. In our sin and brokenness, we couldn't climb up to reach Him, so He climbed down to us and made a perfect way for us to know Him. The shed blood of Jesus unlocked the door for us to be reconciled to God. A royal, heavenly WELCOME mat greets every man, woman, and child who approaches Him through faith in Jesus. We are invited to boldly come in and dine for hours with Him.

Knowing that such a One is pursuing us, it is natural to

want to clear your calendar to spend time often with this heavenly celebrity. I can't conceive of a higher compliment. As we commune with Him, all anxiety vanishes. He reminds us of the words of Jesus. He enlightens us with the "inside scoop" on things happening around us from an eternal perspective. Then, when we leave the dining table, He doesn't stay behind but gets up to accompany us wherever we go. We have become His dwelling place, His living room, His home-sweet-home. This is the unfathomable destiny of every believer.

Back to Jesus' announcement to his disciples about Him leaving and that it was *really* better for them because He was sending the Counselor to them. His disciples weren't ready to fully understand that just yet. Still, Jesus continued unfolding to them what they could expect from this "One called alongside to help." "When He comes, He will *guide you into all truth*. He will not speak on His own; He will speak only what He hears, and He will *tell you what is to come*," John 16:13. "He, the Comforter-Encourager, will *teach you all things* and *remind you* of everything I have said to you," John 14:26. The disciples were no doubt impressed by this resume and perhaps satisfied for the moment. They would understand the rest after they experienced firsthand the outpouring of this promised Spirit at the upcoming feast of Pentecost.

What an extravagant gift. Sent to help us grasp the

mysteries of God, the Holy Spirit reveals to us God's plans and purposes and empowers us to fulfill them. He encourages us, reminding us of the Father's intimate and everlasting love, of the work of the cross, and of our right standing now in Him. He repeats heaven's truths and songs of grace to our hearts and delivers timely insights wherever we need them. He is our ultimate personal coach, counselor, guide, and motivator.

Who doesn't love being around people who inspire? "To inspire" means "to exhilarate, to cheer, to gladden, and imbue with inspiring ideas." How stunning it is to realize that this is what the Holy Spirit came to do for us every day. *He is our greatest source for living up, no matter the circumstances.* No wonder the apostle Paul gives this benediction in his letter to the church in Corinth.

"The *grace* of the Lord Jesus Christ and the *love* of God and the *fellowship* of the Holy Spirit be with you all." The Message translation conveys it this way: "The amazing grace of the Master, Jesus Christ, the extravagant love of God, the intimate friendship of the Holy Spirit, be with all of you." The Trinity covers *all* our bases for an abundant life of impacting our world.

How much more intimate can our friendship with the Holy Spirit be? Let's intentionally clear our calendars more to interact face to face with Him to receive the timely inspiration and encouragement He wants to impart. Let's press on to know Him better and experience everything He was sovereignly sent to do in our lives.

A Practical Application: Understanding His Crazy Plan

I recall a beautiful time when He counseled and enlightened me in a time of confusion. Sitting on the floor of our living room, taping our possessions into boxes, I complained to Him. "Why is it that just when our new church community begins to grow and thrive, and I finally feel like I have roots, You give us a brand new assignment somewhere else? It bothers me. Why can't we stick around to enjoy some of the fruit of these sweet vineyards we've worked so hard to grow? I don't want to leave and start all over again."

Labeling the last few boxes, I recounted this pattern in our lives of laying a foundation for a church or project, then being called to a new "construction site." I wondered if there was something wrong with us...was it just wanderlust?

In the five years since we left our home in Missouri, we had helped birth new church families in several towns. We had made great new friends in the process and helped train new leaders to take over these budding ministries. Now we were leaving again...this time to travel around the world to research the needs of front-line workers in several countries.

I remembered a scripture passage I was studying, promising that the Holy Spirit was given to us to comfort and personally help and guide us. Complaining was getting me nowhere fast, so I decided to take God up on this promise. "Okay, I know you have heard my questions and objections, Holy Spirit, but this is really disturbing me. How about some understanding, counsel, and advice here?" I voiced this request, and then quietly waited in the pile of brown boxes, expecting an explanation.

He dropped an unusual word into my mind: "nomenclature." Having a degree in English, I realized that the Holy Spirit, intimately acquainted with all my ways, was using my love of language to answer me. Loving the intrigue, I sat up to analyze. "Nomenclature, what does that signify?" I got up to get my dictionary (way before cell phones were around) and sensed the Lord smiling at this very personal interplay. The definition of nomenclature jumped out off the page: "the name you are called by." Wow, He was trying to get something to me. Eliminating my first name, I went on to my last name, Porter. The definition of Porter read "one who opens doors for others." A light turned on inside.

I threw the packing tape across the room. "We are Porters. Right. OK, I get it! We are designed to be those who in some way 'open doors for others." I laughed out loud. So there *was* a purpose for our roaming. Once we open doors, others could pass through. That's what pioneers do; they open doors for the next passengers to pass through. The decoding of this fascinating, secret, love note from Him was exhilarating...and very encouraging. Asking the Holy Spirit for His perspective works and *really* enlightens the heart. A sense of peace and security about our seemingly gypsy journey set in deeply. We had done our part and hopefully left a legacy behind, launching other servants to step into their places.

This one word from heaven was caffeine to my spirit. It gave me the knowledge I desperately needed. Seeing our life map from an eternal point of view released the energy I craved to face the next commission. I still cried while hugging friends goodbye, but knew deep down that all this was a part of His plan. I had a divine assurance that we would *always* be forging a new path, dynamiting through new mountains, making new roads because it's our "nomenclature." I determined to pursue His counsel more often.

God's Spirit has something gladdening to say to us today. His very Name is the Encourager. His Word is full of rock-solid promises and wisdom. He has a reminder to give us, an inspiring thought, a compliment, or a revelation to impart. Let's clear our calendars, make a date, and intentionally spend time with this amazing, uplifting Friend. Miraculous moments await us. This offer of love is like *none* other: the indwelling presence in our life of Love Himself. It is through this eternal connection and union with God the Holy Spirit that we are *never* alone or abandoned. He is the power we desperately require to fulfill the high call of service in each one of our lives. What can compare to this privilege of communing with the One who created all things, whose words echo throughout eternity and never return void? This is how you can face every challenge, connected with Deity!

The grace of the Lord Jesus Christ,
and the love of God,
and the fellowship of the Holy Spirit,
be with you all,
-2 Corinthians 13:14.

BONUS BOOSTER

Read and meditate upon this "seated us in heavenly places" mystery confirmed here again in the Passion translation of Colossians 3: 1-3, and marvel.

Christ's resurrection is your resurrection too. This is why we are to yearn for all that is above, for that's where Christ sits enthroned at the place of all power, honor, and authority! Yes, feast on all the treasures of the heavenly realm and fill your thoughts with heavenly realities, and not with the distractions of the natural realm. Your crucifixion with Christ has severed the tie to this life, and now your true life is hidden away in God in Christ. And as Christ himself is seen for who he really is, who you really are will also be revealed, for you are now one with him in his glory!

This is an analogy that is helpful. Just as a President or Prime Minister has been "seated" in a high position with the authority of the office, their work involves traveling and executing the responsibilities of the office while not physically sitting in the appointed office. But everywhere they go, they carry the authority of the position and represent their "kingdom." So it is with believers, we are seated in Christ in heavenly places, but operate in the physical realm on earth. Still everywhere we go, we carry the power and the mandates of the kingdom, representing Him in all we do. We are ambassadors in the truest sense. What an honor.

Small-Group Discussion – Journal Reflections

THREE: HOOK UP TO the GREATEST ENCOURAGER OF ALL TIME

Answer with a friend, a group, or individually in a journal.

1. Talk over why Jesus said it was better for Him to leave them

2. Discuss what you learned about who the Holy Spirit is and what He came to provide for us.

3. Share an experience you have had when you recognized some activity of the Holy Spirit in your life.

4. What are some safeguards for discerning true spiritual guidance or activity in our lives?

5. Discuss how more communion with Him throughout your day could bless your life.

6. Put on some soothing instrumental music and then have a time of quiet fellowship with the Holy Spirit. Allow time for listening as well. Jot down the impressions that came to you. Share.

5

HOW TO KEEP UP WHEN YOU FEEL LIKE GIVING UP

The Almost Missed Miracle & The Little Broom

Nothing great is ever achieved without much enduring.
-St. Catherine of Siena

Without much enduring... If one lives long enough, the truth of this quote resonates loudly. How we loathe waiting, enduring, then waiting some more. But the powerful combination of faith and perseverance is the conduit by which we inherit what He promises. Hebrews chapter six, verse twelve reveals this clearly: "So that you may not be sluggish, but imitators of those who through faith *and* endurance inherit the promises. We need His enCOURAGEment which is the enabling power to stand, *not* give up or give in. It is the "heart-strength to venture, persevere and resist in order to gain concrete results."

Our story of adoption and my husband's story from the wreckage at Ground Zero after the 911 terrorist attack on New York both illustrate this so well. The persevering reward of walking with Him in the encouragement zone when things go wrong is loudly amplified. If we want to see His miracles unfold, we can't afford to give up under pressure. When I hear people say, "I just want to give up," I reply, "and what will you gain then?"

The Almost Missed Miracle

"The photo of your Chinese daughter has arrived!" announced our adoption agency contact. Within minutes, we were driving, drunk with anticipation, our hearts dancing out of our chests toward this magnificent moment.

After fifteen, torturous months of waiting, we glimpsed our first look at the thumb-nail-sized, black and white photo of the little girl destined to be our daughter. "She is," I sighed, "a portrait of innocence."
"She has a cleft palate," the worker reported, "There will

be no way to determine the severity of her condition or how many surgeries she might need until you have her examined."

"Will you accept this match?" he asked.

My mind floated back to the intense crucible we faced in our journey to adopt. Halfway through the process, the Chinese government shocked us by decreeing that families who had children didn't qualify to adopt a healthy child. With two teenage children, this new twist meant that we could only adopt a child with medical needs.

Collapsed in the newly pastel-decorated nursery, I cried "Why this, God?" It had been hard enough, now in our 40s, to rally the courage to adopt a healthy child. My trek through the minefields of fear intensified exponentially.

"I just want my baby, not this nightmare! There are hundreds of thousands of healthy, abandoned girls in China needing families. This red tape is so unfair!" Several families dropped out of the adoption process at this point, disgusted by this new obstacle. "God, help me process this," I agonized.

I traced the heart steps and raw facts that had moved me in the beginning.

"They are killing the baby girls in China!" I exploded at the dinner table to my husband and shocked teenagers.

"The imposed "one child" law for population control has caused a modern holocaust of baby girls."

"Why?" demanded my son, unable to grasp the nonsense.

"Most families want a son for social security and for carrying on the family name, it's a deeply held value in their society," I tried to explain.

"Girls that escape abortion and make it through the birth canal, face another horror: total abandonment," I added, as forks were dropped from hands around the table in disbelief.

"We've got to rescue one of those babies, no matter what the cost."

Self-pity began to diminish as I remembered those words. I pictured new mothers throughout China, just hours after cutting the umbilical cord, being forced to do the unthinkable...and the illegal... to abandon their newborn daughters. I imagined them wiping their tears as they secretly and gently laid their bundled, little girls somewhere out in the open, hoping that the cries of their delicate offspring would be heard... that someone would deliver them to a government welfare institute. Their desperation engulfed me as I envisioned them giving their final kiss.

How could I turn back now? Some precious, tiny girl had miraculously survived the gauntlet of life thus far and awaited my loving arms...would I too, forsake her because she's not physically perfect? I couldn't.

"Yes!" I blurted out loudly to our agency worker, elated that we had settled the issue months earlier.

"You'll fly to meet her in two weeks," he announced to our utter shock.

Our hearts nearly stopped when we sighted the Chinese nannies filing into our Nanchang City hotel lobby, carrying our little bundles.

"Porter," a man called out, signaling that it was our turn to finally meet our baby daughter. He placed a fragile as porcelain masterpiece of a child into my arms. Her black eyes studied me. Our hearts attached as mother and child in one holy second.

Stroking her shaved head marked with insect bites and scratches, all we could say was how beautiful she was. Our little Hannah let us pass her back and forth, mother to father, then brother to sister. Her ebony eyes beckoned as if to say, “Take me, I’m yours.”

Morning light revealed a wonder that overwhelmed us all, an almost missed miracle. I was holding my breath, anxious about what the doctor who was examining Hannah’s tiny cleft palate would have to say.

“How bad is it?”

“Her palate is perfectly normal.”

Our deep sighs and shocked expressions turned to laughter as we realized that there would be no need for surgeries and life-long speech therapy after all. The Great Physician had somehow taken care of all that on His own. We praised Him ardently for our “almost-missed miracle.”

Keeping up when all the circumstances want to suck you under is extremely vital. This story reverberates with that truth. I can’t begin to conceive of the incredible loss to our lives it would have been to have given up the fight. The extreme blessing of knowing and raising our daughter, Hannah, now a bright and world-changing young lady is a treasure beyond measure.

The flip side of that is the stark reality of what might have happened to her. A sick infant, losing weight, the odds for her survival were not in her favor. If she had lived and wasn’t adopted like so many multitudes of babies at that time, her future would have been quite dismal. Older orphans are given adult chores of cleaning toilets, scrubbing floors, and feeding babies while watching others leave for forever families elsewhere. Grown orphans "age out" of the orphanage care at just fourteen years old. They are often thrust out on the street into homelessness, with no real skills or identity to make a life. Orphans are considered "cursed" and "unlucky" and are avoided and spurned by schools and employers. A cultural disdain for these non-persons in society leaves them twice abandoned, without hope. My heart gasps in horror when I think of what dire options Hannah might have faced if we had become discouraged and quit our pursuit to get her. Today she is a college graduate, married, and enjoying a life of opportunity and purpose.

The Bible tells you it takes both faith and patience to realize your goals. When it gets really hard, remember to look to Him and refuse to let go. Someone's life might just depend on it.

Fast forward four years and the little life we brought home brought to my husband *just what he needed to keep going* while working on the rubble pile at Ground Zero, in New York.

The Little Broom Story

(An excerpt from *Destroying the Shadow Agenda*)

Bruce Porter

I was standing on the World Trade Center wreckage in a drizzling rain watching a giant crane pull a twisted steel girder from the rubble. Parts of it glowed red-hot from the raging fires still burning underneath the debris. All of us standing around watched intently, for it was when the jangled mess was disturbed that human remains could be revealed and recovered. When we spotted remains, the work instantly stopped so we could recover whatever we could find. These were placed in a bio-hazard bag and taken immediately to a nearby tent morgue to begin the process of genetic testing for identification. Obviously, this was gruesome smelly work, and it wasn't too unusual to see a SAR (Search and Rescue) worker hunched over retching.

It was early evening on the fifth day of my service in New York City, and darkness slowly enveloped Lower Manhattan. The work would go on throughout the night. The size and scope of the destruction were almost too much for the mind to take in. Banks of bright searchlights illuminated enormous plumes of smoke and steam rising from the debris, creating an eerie, otherworldly effect to the scene. I glanced around at helmeted men and women, representing various agencies from all over the nation, as they climbed around on the pile performing various duties. A couple of ironworkers positioned high up on the rubble in a basket suspended from a towering crane cut away parts of the tangled wreckage with acetylene torches. This created multi-colored fountains of bright sparks that cascaded down on the rubble below. The unspeakable horror all around me and the beautiful and ethereal showers of sparks created a weird contrast.

I stood there wondering how long the search for human remains, and perhaps even a survivor, would go on. Indeed, it would continue through this long rainy night until the dawn, and likely for many more dawnings to come. For some of these people who lost friends and loved ones in this jumble of wreckage, the desperate search would continue at some deeper emotional level for the rest of their lives. Such scenes become imprinted upon the mind and heart and would remain with us all forever. No eraser but the grace of God could ever cleanse the mind of such terrible scenes.

In the midst of this milieu, I suddenly heard the faint electronic ringing of my cell phone tucked inside my grimy, rain-drenched turnout jacket. Groping for the phone, I finally pulled it up to my ear, only to be frustrated by my breathing mask strapped over my mouth and nose.

Jerking the mask down so I could speak, I heard my voice say in a barely audible croak, "Hello?"

Over the noise of machinery, and the hissing of torches and generators, I could faintly discern a small child's voice on the phone say; ì Daddy, what are you dooo-ing? I instantly recognized the voice of my five-year-old Hannah. She was watching the live 24-hour televised feed of Ground Zero at home back in Colorado. She'd been looking for a glimpse of me there. I heard her say, "Where are you, Daddy? I can't see you." My heart melted.

Her sweet voice instantly drew me back into a much happier place that seemed now only a dim memory. She was calling out to me from her childish world where all things were good, safe, and peaceful. Her days were filled listening to Winnie the Pooh stories or watching colorful birds visit our bird feeder or staring at clouds while trying to decide what kind of animal they resembled. I ached with all my heart to be back in her world again. Her voice was like a cold drink of water in a dry and dusty desert.

Standing there in the rain, with heavy equipment clanking all around me, I struggled for several moments to respond to her question. What could I say to answer my little girl's question without alarming her? I knew that soon enough the harsher realities of this broken world would hurt her, and perhaps even break her heart. I desperately wanted to protect her and knew I had to choose my words carefully.

I could hear her breathing into the phone, patiently waiting for me to answer her question. My eyes swept over the smoldering wreckage surrounding me where untold thousands of people lay mangled in smoking rubble. Finally, I said, "Honey, some mean bad guys made a big mess here in New York City, and I'm just helping to clean it up."

There was a pregnant pause on the phone as she thought about this. Then, in her sweet, innocent voice, she replied:

"Daddy, can I bring my little broom and help?"

The power of her question struck me like a bolt of lightning. I froze, and for several moments I couldn't speak past the enormous lump forming in my throat. The emotions that welled up were like a volcanic eruption I'd held in check until that moment. Choking back sobs, I finally gained enough control to respond. I don't remember what I said exactly, but only recall mumbling something about how important it was that she uses her little broom to help mommy clean up the messes there at home. It was nearly impossible to suppress my emotions. With a husky voice, I thanked her for calling and offering to help. I told her I loved her, promising to call back as soon as I could before ending the call.

Slipping the phone back into a pocket, I pulled up my protective mask back over my mouth and nose. Despite my best efforts to keep it together, my knees buckled and I plopped down in the rubble sobbing like a baby. My little girl had just expressed as clearly as human language could ever communicate what I, and most likely everyone around me, felt in this horrible place. For whatever training and willingness to serve I possessed, all I felt I'd managed to bring to this hell-hole was a little broom. What was that compared to the millions of tons of twisted wreckage, shattered dreams, and broken hearts? The disaster was so enormous and overwhelming, nothing I did seemed to make any difference. This feeling of helplessness was especially true since we couldn't find anyone alive.

For several minutes, I battled a wave of depression sweeping over me. It felt like I was sinking into a pit of despair like a fissure opened up under me in the rubble. In this dark place, I fought for breath, hope, and for faith. Only love held me up–the love of a little girl in Colorado who called her daddy to make sure he was okay. Her call was a lifeline of love, and I clung to it with all my strength.

At that moment of the deepest depression, I desperately cried out to God. "Jesus, I'm so weak and useless, and the needs here are so great. Please help me." A powerful revelation suddenly flooded my mind. In that instant, I was reminded this situation was not the slightest bit about me. Rather, it was about the tens of thousands of brokenhearted children and parents and husbands and wives and friends in a traumatized city who were facing a long future of crying themselves to sleep night after night. It was about people longing for someone they loved, who would never come home again, ever. It was about people looking up every day at a gaping hole in their skyline, bereft of the gleaming towers, and having to relive over and over the memory of that horrible day in September.

The loud metallic clanking of one of the cranes dragging another massive chunk of twisted metal out of the rubble pulled me out of the debris of my dark brooding, and back into the moment. Scrambling to my feet, and feeling a little embarrassed about my emotional display, I wiped the tears from my face with a grimy glove and looked around. The guys nearby seemed to ignore me, pressing into the work at hand, but I'm sure that they understood how I was feeling and could relate. Some things don't need much explanation in the brotherhood of suffering.

I wandered back toward the makeshift tent morgue near the World Financial Center. I thought again of the medical and support teams in there who were enduring the task of processing and cataloging the body parts we were bringing in. A weeping Firefighter Chaplain would once again take his little broom in there for a while, and try to comfort, encourage, and sweep away some of the mess. A little broom, I reminded myself, can do something useful and make a difference when made available. Even my little girl was smart enough to know that.

If you wait until you can do everything for everybody,
instead of doing something for somebody,
you'll end up not doing anything for anybody.
-Malcolm Bane

Follow the Divine Instincts of Your Heart

Our Lord imprints *specific* compassion into our hearts as a clear signpost of His will in our lives. "For God is working in you, giving you the desire and the power to do what He pleases," Philippians 2:13, the New Living Translation. Notice and pay close attention to what breaks your heart in this world and realize that He is going to use you in some way to address that very wound. I can trace His guidance toward loving Chinese children and caring for orphans back to the experience of leading singing at the children's crusade in Taiwan. Later, my heartbreak for the abandoned baby girls in China was the next God clue that He was prompting me to venture toward and take action. What could I do to help the multiple millions of delicate infants perishing? I remembered the words of a dear friend who adopted a daughter from Korea years ago, "If every

Christian family would adopt just one child, think how the kingdom of God would be impacted." I knew this was the time to act and the rest is history. It took His divine COURAGE to adopt Hannah every step of the way. Yet the call to touch more orphans and vulnerable children continued to grow. One obedience leads to another assignment. As the wise saying about the two ingredients for success says, "Get started and don't quit."

Divine Appointments for Children in Africa

"Desperate women in my country often cast their babies into the trash and pit latrines"

While speaking at a women's conference in England, I met a beautiful black woman attending from Uganda. During a luncheon, I felt drawn to go over and talk with her about how to assist orphans in her country. She divulged some unforgettable and cruel facts. "Many women are hopeless and desperate in my country... often they cast their newborn babies into the trash and pit latrines." Her eyes filled with tears as she continued in a low, compassionate voice. "Recently in my own neighborhood,

James 1:27 had been shouting to my spirit for months, "Religion that God our Father accepts as pure and faultless is this: to look after orphans and widows in distress and to keep oneself unstained by the world."

my children, on their way to buy a loaf of bread were screaming hysterically as they witnessed a wild dog devouring a dead baby who was left on the road." At this point, we were both gulping back sobs. She informed me that in Uganda, "There are no government funds available to rescue children or support homes for them, none. The future of these babies rests solely in the hands of those whose hearts and hands are moved to help."

I sat quietly, sensing that God was speaking. "Well, I guess that would be me," I said. "I don't have the money personally, but I can be a voice for these kids to my family and friends in America. With God's help, hearts will be moved to save these perishing ones." I took that first, scary step with which *every* important journey begins. I knew in my heart that we had to build a safe home for them. James 1:27 had been shouting to my spirit for months, "Religion that God our Father accepts as pure and faultless is this: to look after orphans and widows in distress and to keep oneself unstained by the world." I offered myself to Him to be a voice for the sake of these outcast babies. To the world, they might be trash, but to God, they are invaluable treasures. He would make a way for their lives to be saved. I was confident that He was working to will and to work His good pleasure in and through this divine appointment.

A long story made short, the momentum to rescue

these helpless ones spread through my circles like a long row of dominoes falling upon one another creating a catalyst of compassion and action. Children, family members, close friends, teenagers, teachers, moms, dads, and grandparents began to respond to the call for help. Friends told friends who told other friends. Benefit concerts, ladies' teas, garage sales, spaghetti dinners, hand-knit baby blankets, and baked goods sales spontaneously multiplied and amplified the cries of the newborns. School mission projects and philanthropic heroes stepped forward in solidarity. Soon, we purchased acres of lush land, and a sweet haven baby home was built. Everyone working together, PERSEVERING and TAKING COURAGE through challenge after challenge resulted in over seventy "treasures" being rescued and many finding forever homes. Joy is the invaluable reward that results from laying your life down for those who can never repay you. That extraordinary beginning continues to bless lives, and continuous miraculous stories unfold.

Relentless Love in the Slums of Nairobi

"There is no exercise better for the heart than reaching down and lifting people up," John Andrew Holmes

What kind of poor, single woman raising a toddler starts a school for hundreds of children living in the slums of Nairobi, Kenya? One who knows how to *persevere* and fulfill her destiny by the power of enCOURAGEment!

Merriam Webster defines *persevering* as "continuing despite difficulties, opposition, or discouragement." That perfectly describes my beloved Kenyan friend, Hellen, with whom I am currently partnering. Hellen was born into a large family in a mountain village. Daughter of a freedom fighter in the bloody Mau Mau uprising against British rule in the 1950s, Hellen fights for a different kind of freedom: an educational opportunity for the poorest of the poor in the slums of Nairobi. The traumatic event of being abandoned by her husband to raise their toddler with no support led to Hellen's powerful encounter with Jesus Christ and a vision to use her educational training as a teacher to lift the most vulnerable.

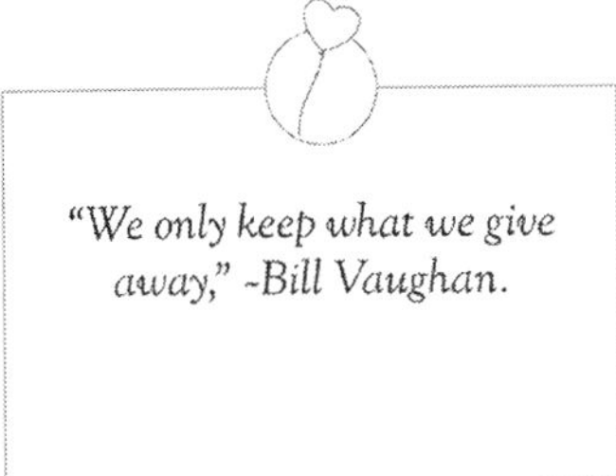

Petra School on the Rock started with 8 street children learning in the makeshift tin shack Hellen constructed on a dirt floor with rustic benches. Hellen happily endured those conditions knowing what she did "for the least of these" she was doing unto Jesus. More and more slum children peered into the shack in hopes of getting a chance at an education. Hellen used trashed metal sheets to create new sections for them. Years later, through faith and patience, multiplied hundreds of children receive their divine tickets out of extreme poverty through the ministry of Petra School on the Rock, then housed in a larger, old building leased by Hellen.

When I visited this 50ft by 50ft two-story school in 2018, truly overflowing with beautiful students from pre-school to grade 8, my "God-pager" went off in my heart again and I knew our ministry, Torchgrab Africa, was to help. Over 50% of kids living in nearby slums NEVER get to school and become slaves to a life of trafficking, drugs, abuse, and disease. We determined that we could change that by endeavoring to buy land and construct a four-story, second Petra School on the Rock near and for these defenseless and endangered children. After all, "We only keep what we give away," Bill Vaughan.

Even during the Covid pandemic shutdowns, we *refused to give up* and Hellen's dream, now our's too, kept taking on flesh. We were able to feed many families who were unemployed and without any food during these lockdowns while continuing to build the new school one cement brick at a time. As soon as the lockdown ended, the new Petra school staff came ready to teach the growing flock of eager orphans and slum-dwelling boys and girls who filled the classrooms of the finished first floor, even in the midst of construction all around. Rain blew through into the classes through the unfinished windows, but the teachers and students were unmoved.

Refusing to be stopped in our efforts to bring a team to

Nairobi after the shutdown in 2020, our Torchgrab Africa team of twenty-one kept preparing and traveled the instant the doors opened again. We brought wellness training, a vacation Bible school teaching series, and built a clean water filtration system for Petra kids, now nearly 1,000 strong in multiple locations. The miracle continues and soon we will dedicate this life-saving new school with four stories of classrooms and an unheard-of actual library, music room, and future computer lab. Now, the slum children of Nairobi can rise up, take their own little brooms and bring hope and healing to their nation.

"Those who are happiest are those who do the most for others," Booker T. Washington. May these stories be an inspiration to all readers from every station and circumstance to take courage, *press onward,* and keep UP no matter the cost. Great things *do* come from "much enduring." And each victory leads to the next! The power to complete our assignments comes supernaturally from Him. Lives in the present and in the future are *depending on you* to answer your call, take up your "little broom" and never give up.

BONUS BOOSTER

The magnificence of the work of Jesus and the love of God for us is the foundation of all UP-living.

Because you are in Christ:

In the mind of God, you have already, in the past, been redeemed and totally forgiven for every sin because of Christ.

Rejoice that you can add NOTHING to His sacrifice to make you more pleasing to God. Condemnation is finished. Imputed righteousness is forever!

Small-Group Discussion – Journal Questions
FOUR: KEEP UP EVEN WHEN YOU FEEL LIKE GIVING UP

Answer with a friend, a group, or individually in a journal.

1. Do you view perseverance with a little less groaning now and more positivity? Why?

2. What does "The Little Broom" story message mean to you?

3. Read and put into your own words Hebrews 6:12.

4. Share a time when you felt like giving up but persevered to see His results.

5. Share a present challenge you are facing in which you need His strength to persevere and pray for one another regarding those challenges.

6

HOW TO FILL UP WITH THE CREATIVE FORCE OF JOY

Guard your joy and it will guard you

Every facet of living UP is interrelated like the spokes of a bicycle wheel. Joy is a *huge* and *serious* subject.

Joy is *not* a frivolous novelty intended only for those happy-go-lucky, bluebird temperaments or rare lottery winners. Joy gives the buoyancy you need to float above despondency. It is a creative force designed to empower every wayfaring traveler who is passing through this "world of woe," as the folk song aptly states. You *gotta* have it.

I love accessories...shiny earrings, bright, textured scarves, and matching jewelry accents that jazz up an otherwise plain outfit. But these embellishments are not essential; I can hear very well without my sparkling earrings. And in the same way, colorfully designed phone cases are distinguished as a fashion statement, but phones work *without* a fancy case, as long as they charge regularly. So it is with our lives...

Many of us treat the presence of joy and encouragement in our lives kind of like we do those accessories, as totally optional, or worse, as just an unattainable fantasy. We rationalize that joy is fleeting and we have learned to cope without it. Having lasting joy is relegated to a rare and extraordinary experience reserved only for very special occasions, a dream vacation cruise, or a lucky coincidence.

Oh, we all know how to put on a happy face for the obligatory show of cheeriness when appropriate, but when we are alone, the fog of discontent and gloom so easily sets in. We've lived so long with this emotional haze that it is strangely comforting in its familiarity. Content to live in a seems-like-normal state of melancholy or at best apathy, we live joy-deprived most of our days...mostly because we don't know how to live any differently. We agree that "Life is pain, and anyone who says anything different is selling something," William Golden, author of *The Princess Bride*. This chapter challenges that false belief. Suffering happens, yes, but staying in pain is a choice.

No one has *ever* died of an overdose of encouragement

Imagine a headline reading, "Masses of people die of too much encouragement and an overdose of laughter. Psychologists urged to make sure clients have more depression in their lives to balance the excessive joy."

Absurd, right? Too much encouragement is not a problem. Rather, a severe and sinister epidemic of despondency has crept into millions of our lives like a noxious, invisible gas. This malevolence seeks to slime us and it works like deathly quicksand to pull us under. Like a drained cell phone, we slowly go dark without a daily recharge of divine, God-infused joy. God's joy releases an essential spiritual vitality; **it is heaven's anti-depressant.** Millions of people battle the devouring thief called depression. It strangles energy, assassinates hope, and steals potential.

According to a Web MD article about the effects of depression on other illnesses, "Depression increases your risk of a number of diseases and other conditions by, for example, increasing levels of stress hormones such as cortisol or adrenaline. Depression can affect the immune system, making it harder for our body to fight infection.

Some vaccinations such as the shingles vaccine may even be less effective in older adults with depression. Depression has also been linked to heart disease and increased risk for substance abuse."[1]

Ingesting joy is a life-and-death issue. We can't afford a cavalier attitude toward it. So, no matter what our present joy level is, I am striving to unfold ways it can be significantly increased in our lives. And not superficially.

Why Bother?

Medical studies concur that sad-hearted living negatively impacts our health, but cheerfulness actually boosts our immune system. A Harvard Medical School Health Digest article asserts: "Want to feel better and improve your health? Start by focusing on the things that bring you happiness. Scientific evidence suggests that positive emotions can help make life longer and healthier." This confirms what is stated in the Bible in the book of Proverbs. The ancient book of wisdom has all along contained the ancient secret linking the relationship between joy and health, discouragement and death. Several translations that follow open up the literal meaning of Proverbs 17:22.

1. https://www.webmd.com/depression/how-depression-affects-your-body#1-3

A cheerful heart is good medicine, but a crushed spirit *dries up the bones.* (NIV)

A cheerful heart is good medicine, but a broken spirit *saps a person's strength.* (NLT)

A *joyful heart is good medicine*, but a crushed spirit dries up the bones. (ESV)

A *merry heart doeth good like a medicine*: but a broken spirit drieth the bones. (KJV)

If you are cheerful, you feel good; *if you are sad, you hurt all over*. (CEV)

Being cheerful *keeps you healthy*. It is *a slow death to be gloomy all the time.* (GNT)

A joyful, cheerful heart *brings healing to both body and soul.* But the *one whose heart is crushed struggles with sickness and depression.* (TPT)

The obvious corollary is that if we want to stay healthy, we cannot divorce joy from our life. We naturally want health, strength, and long life. Both the scriptures and medical science layout the inseparable connection between our emotional well-being and our ultimate physical well-being.

I list some of the many benefits of laughter contained in an article from Laughter is the Best Medicine.[2]

Laughter is good for your health.

Laughter relaxes the whole body. A good, hearty laugh relieves physical tension and stress, leaving your muscles relaxed for up to forty-five minutes.

Laughter boosts the immune system.

Medical studies concur that sad-hearted living negatively impacts our health, but cheerfulness actually boosts our immune system.

Laughter decreases stress hormones and increases immune cells and infection-fighting antibodies, thus improving your resistance to disease.

Laughter triggers the release of endorphins, the body's natural feel-good chemicals. Endorphins promote an overall sense of well-being and can even temporarily relieve pain.

Laughter protects the heart.

Laughter improves the function of blood vessels and increases blood flow, which can help protect you against a heart attack and other cardiovascular problems.

2. https://www.helpguide.org/articles/mental-health/laughter-is-the-best-medicine.htm.

Laughter burns calories. OK, so it's no replacement for going to the gym, but one study found that laughing for 10 to 15 minutes a day can burn about 40 calories—which could be enough to lose three or four pounds over the course of a year.

Laughter lightens anger's heavy load. Nothing diffuses anger and conflict faster than a shared laugh. Looking at the funny side can put problems into perspective and enable you to move on from confrontations without holding onto bitterness or resentment.

Laughter may even help you to live longer. A study in Norway found that people with a strong sense of humor outlived those who don't laugh as much. The difference was particularly notable for those battling cancer. The bottom line is that, as Proverbs stated, there are *significant* physical health benefits from laughter.

"Sometimes your joy is the source of your smile, but sometimes your smile can be the source of your joy." —Thich Nhat Hanh

Did you know there is a physical benefit from smiling? A simple smile releases neuropeptides that relieve stress and increases endorphins. Activate these health lifters with an intentional smile throughout your days.[3]

Again, science confirms the truth of this proverb that joy is literally a vital life force, a "medicine" and a powerful influence in physical healing. The second part of this verse in Proverbs 17:22 is just as astounding in its implication. "A broken spirit or depressed heart *dries the bones*." This is not an empty, poetic metaphor, but a reference to an alarming medical reality.

What important operation takes place in our bones?

The production of healthy blood cells occurs in the bone marrow. Bone marrow is a spongy substance found in the center of the bones. It manufactures stem cells and other substances, which in turn produce blood cells. Each type of blood cell made by the bone marrow has an important job. Red blood cells carry oxygen to tissues in the body. Platelets help the blood to clot in order to stop bleeding. White blood cells fight infections. NO, we don't want our bones to "dry." That would stop the very life-producing process that keeps you alive and well.[4]

3. https://www.psychologytoday.com/us/blog/cutting-edge-leadership/201206/there-s-magic-in-your-smile
4. https://www.sciencedaily.com/terms/bone_marrow.htm

In laymen's terms, the ancient scriptures reveal what scientists and medical research have now established: on some very basic level, unchallenged, chronic discouragement *kills us.* Joy and encouragement bring physical and emotional healing. The research of Dr. Caroline Leaf in her book *Who Switched Off My Brain* reveals that "87% to 95% of the illnesses that plague you today are a direct result of our thought life. "What we think about affects us physically and emotionally. It's an epidemic of toxic emotions."

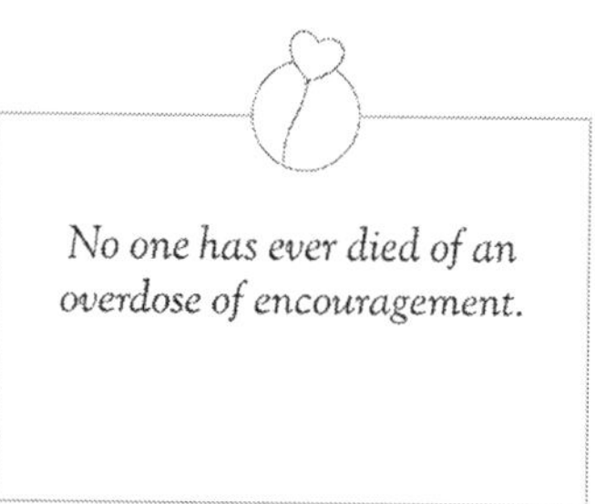

No one has ever died of an overdose of encouragement.

Important volumes have been written about depression, but *so very little* about joy. This chapter is devoted to uncovering secrets about how to ingest this creative force and heavenly antidepressant.

For those reading who are in the midst of a difficult depression, I do not presume to speak as a doctor or psychiatrist or to present a shallow formula that might further depress you. I hope to compassionately share some small encouraging glimpses that will bring comfort and available resources that will aid in your recovery. For others, I wish to impart some tools that will help you establish beneficial safeguards against the ongoing plague of discouragement.

Understanding Biblical Joy

Our Hollywood or fairy tale concept of joy is often associated with the acquisition of a new sports car, a silkier shampoo, the ideal lifestyle, a new romance, a successful career, or a bucket-list vacation.

Biblical joy has little to do with outer circumstances or possessions. It is not determined by or isolated to the fleeting attainment of status or fame. It surpasses any past or present circumstances and isn't created by feast or limited by famine. This is a liberating reality when grasped. We can experience this unique kind of joy no matter *what* our situation may be.

Understanding that joy is *more* than just a feeling is foundational. Joy, the scripture reveals, is a fruit of His Spirit. Lives that are controlled by or always influenced by emotions are very unstable. My emotions can take me on a roller coaster from euphoria to the depths of despair all within half an hour. My feelings can fluctuate based on my hormones, what I have eaten, how much sleep I've gotten, or what I have been thinking about. I have learned not to be led by those unreliable guides.

This concept can perhaps be better understood when it

is applied to the fruit of love. True love is also *more* than a feeling. Feelings are a part of love, but love is *far* more than feelings. Love, joy, and all the fruit of the Spirit are not temporal or unstable. It is tragic how many couples have judged that because their feelings for one another have fluctuated, love has therefore wavered and vanished. God's kind of love, agape love, is unconditional love. His love never changes because of a mood or a betrayal. He *is* love and always will be. Contrary to common terminology, we can't really "fall into love," nor can we fall out of true love. We can fall in and out of the *feelings* of love, but genuine love exists more solidly beneath the feeling realm.

Biblical love is based on a choice; a commitment to care for another person regardless of the continual presence of those wonderful emotions. Over and over I have experienced that when I act toward my husband in a loving way (without first needing any feeling) loving feelings *often* follow the action. It's not the other way around. Love is a like beautiful cherry tree with deep roots. Feelings are like blossoms and cherries. Once the blossoms and cherries manifest and then disappear in their season, the tree still exists with the potential of more blossoming flowers in the seasons to come. This truth can be a relationship saver and a joy-builder.

Another way to understand this follows. I am a citizen of the United States. You may be a citizen of another country. This is not something you always feel, it is just a fact. Because we don't necessarily "feel" like an American or (name your country) doesn't change the undeniable fact that we *are*. We might awaken some morning and not "feel" like a human. It doesn't change the fact that you are one. In the same way, just because we don't always feel love or joy doesn't mean the facts have changed. His Spirit in us is permanent and unchanging. We can learn to draw on those unchanging resources and expect that feelings will come and go.

It struck me that joy was a Spirit-strengthened choice. I possessed joy without necessarily having to feel it because I possessed Him.

Because of your union with Him, you already have it!

"But the fruit of the Spirit is love, joy, peace," Galatians 5:22. Second only to love, joy is listed as a component of the very nature of God. For those who always picture Him as angry and irritated...here's a different glimpse of a God who smiles, even laughs. The Spirit referred to is God, the Holy Spirit, the part of the Trinity we have been introduced to who is sent to live inside of believers. When a person receives the gift of forgiveness by believing in Christ and His work on the cross, the Bible teaches that his/her human spirit is "born again."

"For you have been born again, not of seed which is perishable, but imperishable, that is, through the living and abiding word of God," 1 Peter 1:23.

In this magnificent new birth, God's own nature is deposited into a believer's new spirit. God, by His Spirit, literally moves in with His entire luggage. I know that sounds unbelievable, but it is true and *real*. He moves into our spirit with all that He is, His love, joy, peace, patience, holiness, wisdom, you name it. We are now able to be transformed into creations in His image and likeness again, with a new and beautiful inner landscape. Ephesians 1:3 reveals that He has blessed us in the heavenly realms with *every* spiritual blessing in Christ. Every means every!

This miracle of new life is the supernatural work of the Holy Spirit, connecting our human spirit once again with the nature of God Himself. A fresh line of communication is established and an ever-growing relationship with the heavenly Father God is 100% available. Our formerly dead spirit, as a result of sin, is made alive, like a new antenna being launched inside of us to receive transmissions from heaven. By His Spirit, He literally comes to us, invading our life with heavenly, eternal contents. Our new DNA includes His very nature. This means we are already filled with a rich, unending deposit of biblical joy, every spiritual blessing, and everything He is. This remains true whether we believe, feel or experience it or not. Live from these eternal facts and discover fresh joy welling up inside. "Selah" is a Hebrew word for "pause and meditate on that." Selah.

Stop Postponing Joy!

Scripture exhorts believers to, "Be continually filled with the Spirit," Ephesians 5:18. This means to *right now* be continually filled with everything the Spirit has. We are promised that because of His Spirit overflowing in us, we can live and walk in a brand new realm, drawing from every rich resource now made available via the Holy Spirit. If we could take a selfie photo of what we look like in our born-again spirit, Galatians 5:22-23 gives a clear description of what we look like. "But the fruit of the Spirit is love, joy, peace, patience, kindness, goodness, gentleness, and self-control." That is not how we will look in the future, but how we look *right now*. As we grow, simply living daily in union with Him, we will naturally produce all the fruit mentioned in this verse as we abide in Him.

God is always love, and He always has an abiding joy. He is never in a bad mood. And everything He is, His seed, His nature, is now inside believers. We can draw from love, joy, peace, and all the fruit of His Spirit *whenever* needed. As I began to see this exciting provision, it hit me that the necessity for prolonged pity parties or bad moods was no longer on the menu for me. Why would I choose to eat dog food when I have access to gourmet dining with the King?

Paul put it this way, "I have been crucified with Christ, and it is no longer I who live, but Christ lives in me; and the life which I now live in the flesh I live by faith in the Son of God, who loved me, and delivered Himself up for me." Galatians 2:20

God has, and we have access. In John chapter 15, Jesus describes us as a branch abiding in Him the Vine. As we dwell in and stay intimately connected to Him, the fruit of the Vine will naturally be reproduced in the branch. Fruit doesn't groan and struggle, it is the natural result of simply abiding in the vine. I have experienced the incredible and unending supply of this source of joy over and over again, even in the midst of extremely painful circumstances. This sounds great, but let me give an example of how this works in real life.

Joy and Worship...an "Up" Lifestyle

I am a musician. Music opens my soul to experience gladness on some level that I can't explain. Expressing love to God in music is a shortcut to joy like nothing else for me. Leading groups of believers in songs and times of worship forced me to learn a great lesson. This half-hour or more, dedicated to singing and giving our full attention to Him, is designed to be a rich and inspiring encounter.

David, a songwriter, and leader in ancient Israel proclaims this experience of joy flowing from his close relationship to God and pleasure while worshiping Him. This treasure is echoed throughout his psalms.

> "You will show me the path of life; In Your presence is the fullness of joy;
> At Your right hand are pleasures forevermore," Psalm 16:11.
> "You make him joyful with gladness in Your presence," Psalm 21-6.
> "Then I will go to the altar of God, to God, my exceeding joy," Psalm 43:4.

Biblical joy has little to do with outer circumstances or possessions.

As a worship leader, my prayer and desire are to facilitate the opportunity for others to experience this fountain of gladness and joy in God's presence. Some of the "mechanics" of this involve choosing and arranging a variety of songs that inspire and lift, in some settings it means practicing with a band of musicians and singers, having great harmonies, getting the sound system to work, and providing visuals with the lyrics for people to see. That's the easy part. These things alone do not ensure a meaningful time of group worship.

My heart attitude, my countenance, and my focus as the leader can color the entire experience. It is imperative that I prepare *myself* to be a vessel of encouragement. The last thing people need is for me to project a sour face, a negative attitude, or a plastic smile upon them. I want to be a carrier of His presence, like the Levites in the old covenant who carried the ark of His presence before the congregation.

Knowing this forced me to spend time with the "Vine," the fountainhead of pleasure before every gathering. I consciously cast my cares, bad attitudes, or anxieties on Him, drawing near to Him in sincere closeness and love. There are *many* times I showed up at a service to lead worship when I didn't feel *at all* like singing and praising Him. I wanted to go home and sulk or ponder whatever problem I was facing. Knowing how selfish that was and the importance of leading worship by first *being* a worshiper, I learned not to yield to those quicksand feelings. I had to dump them before the first note.

I saw distinct changes inside me week after week of practicing this preparation process. After casting my "junk" consistently on the Lord in prayer and simply deciding to give Him my worship, over and over, by the middle of the first song, I noticed my feelings of joy and awe in worship would emerge. I would start out "cold-turkey" to offer my sincere thanks but then found a well of joy springing up from somewhere beyond emotions filling me to overflowing. It was like turning on a shower. His presence would pour through me, lift and cheer me *consistently* when I let my focus be on Him. "So this is how joy operates," I thought. "It really *is* inside me, just waiting to be released as I put my eyes on You and begin to offer You thanks." It struck me that joy was a Spirit-strengthened choice. I possessed joy without *necessarily* having to feel it because I possessed *Him*. That meant I could take a fragrant, therapeutic "shower" in His presence at *any* time. I learned the almost lost art of living UP in joy in order to lift others up!

This has been so radical and wonderfully liberating. Living in joy is not limited to our emotional state, or determined by our environment. The joy of the Lord is a spiritual well *inside* of us, unhindered by our fluctuating dispositions or present conditions. Abiding in this reality, we can draw from His unwavering, unfaltering, and ever-available cascade of joy, 24-7.

Casting *all* your cares on Him

I love this old folk song chorus: "If somehow you could pack up your sorrows and give them all to me. You would lose them, I know how to use them, give them all to me." This invitation is offered to us in this scriptural directive: "Cast *all your cares* on Him because *He cares* for you," 1 Peter 5:7.

Here is an illustration of how you can do this that might help. A Good Will store opened near us. A feature I love is the drive-through dump lane. You drive up to the door, point to your "bags" in the back and a worker takes them out and waves you on with a smile! That's a *great* picture of how we can be transparent and honest and unload our cares and discouragements on the Lord. Just imagine driving up to Him in prayer, acknowledging the things weighing you down, and Him lifting them from you and tossing them aside. Picture Him replacing your anxiety with His peaceful assurance, then smiling and waving you forward. He actually stays in the car with You as you drive off. Then *notice* how an inner contentedness overtakes you.

We don't need to wait for the worship service to unload our depressing trash on the Lord, exchanging it for His beauty and laughter. We can do it *habitually* and therefore enjoy not just isolated moments, but a lifestyle of inner satisfaction and carefree joy.

"The Joy of the Lord is Your Strength," Nehemiah 8:10

I've seen this famous verse on plaques and framed with lovely art, but have wondered how many people realize its potency and significance. We can't separate strength from joy. Until I studied the context of this verse, I had no clue of the magnitude of its importance.

In 427 BC, Nehemiah was inspired by God to leave his comfortable life as a cupbearer and trusted officer to King Artaxerxes I (son of King Artaxerxes who took queen Esther as his wife) to take on the challenge of rebuilding the wall around the burned, conquered and devastated the city of Jerusalem. Given the blessing of the King to begin this great undertaking, Nehemiah (which means "Yahweh comforts" in Hebrew) traveled to inspect the condition of the wall around Jerusalem at night. He mobilized a workforce of Jews amidst many seemingly insurmountable obstacles and threats and successfully completed the massive project in a relatively short time. This effort had colossal repercussions for the nation of Israel.

The mammoth wall around the city, historically, was much more than a nice architectural touch. It was the chief offensive and defensive protection and security for the city. The wall was literally a fortress and a defense for the inhabitants. The rebuilding of the wall around Jerusalem put it back "on the map" so to speak, as a safe and powerful refuge to which the Jews could return. It was a symbol of God's faithfulness and promise to make Jerusalem His city of praise.

The creative force of the joy of the Lord is actually a wall of fortification for our security and well-being.

After the massive wall was completed and people returned to live in Jerusalem, Nehemiah also restored the activities and practices of the Jewish faith. He became governor and established social and religious law and practices according to the scriptures. At the celebration of this miraculous rebuilding of the wall and re-establishment of God's people to the city, he ordered the public reading of scripture before the re-gathered Jews. Scripture tells us that upon hearing the Law read in this significant ceremony, the people began to weep. It is at this momentous occasion that Nehemiah proclaims, "Do not weep any longer, for *the joy of the Lord is your strength*," Nehemiah 8:10.

In order to really understand why the people wept when they heard the Word, we need to understand their situation. Nebuchadnezzar carried away the first inhabitants of Jerusalem in 497 B.C. It is now forty-three years later, 454 B.C. Many of them have been allowed to return to Jerusalem and rebuild. To understand the impact of Nehemiah's statement, we must understand that the Hebrew word "ma`owz" Nehemiah used it for "strength." According to *Strong's Exhaustive Concordance*, the definition of ma-owz is literally "a fortified place; figuratively, a defense:–force, fort(-ress), rock, strength(-en), strong (hold)."

The word "strength" used here in Hebrew is literally

"fortress wall." Imagine what went through the minds of the people who had just risked life and limb to rebuild the wall around Jerusalem, the protective structure around their city. Nehemiah declared to the people that the joy of the Lord was like that "wall," their fortress, their literal shield against danger and conquest. Keep this word picture firmly in your vision. His joy is what is supposed to surround us, fortify and protect us from all incoming enemies. How foolish to think we can live with our wall down!

Not only is the joy of the Lord our strength, but it is a protection of unparalleled power. The creative force of the joy of the Lord is actually a wall of fortification for our security and well-being. Once again, we are faced with the distinctive power of joy in our lives. Not only does it release life and health into our bodies, but it becomes a wall of protection surrounding us, guarding us against attack and conquest. Paul echoes this truth in his letter to the Philippians when he wrote, "Rejoice in the Lord *always*. Again I say, rejoice. To remind you of this is *no* problem for me and it is a *safeguard* for you." The word safeguard also implies protection as does the wall around Jerusalem.

Paul wrote this exhortation from prison, where his conditions were anything but joy-producing. He was drawing from *another* source: the everlasting river flowing from the majestic Joy-Giver which never runs dry. The wall analogy helps us picture joy as absolutely vital, not an accessory in our lives. If we guard our joy by living in refreshing union with Him, His joy will guard us. I hope we are realizing that drawing from the geyser of His joy is not optional, but boosts our health, and our emotional well-being and provides a surrounding wall of protection for us. Every day we can make an effort to include joy-giving moments, songs of worship, and mini-mental vacations looking into His eyes of love to help boost our joy-health. For it literally *is* our fortress and strength and the creative force that electrifies our lives for living UP.

BONUS BOOSTER

In the mind of God, you have already been declared righteous and justified in Christ.

"Being justified freely by His grace through the redemption that is in Christ Jesus," Romans 3:24

Now it's your turn to smile and agree with God and declare that in Him, you have right standing and bold access to His throne. "He who sits in the heavens laughs..." Psalm 2: 4. And the context here is that all the nations are warring against God and His Anointed. So we can imitate Him and increase our joy even in times of battle.

Small-Group Discussion – Journal Questions

FIVE: FILL UP WITH THE CREATIVE FORCE OF JOY

Answer with a friend, a group, or individually in a journal.

1. In what ways is your understanding of joy being expanded in this chapter?

2. What has science and scripture revealed about the importance of joy in our lives?

3. Discuss and recount the many medical benefits associated with a joyous outlook.Explore the concept from Nehemiah that the joy of the Lord is our wall of fortress.

4. What are some practical ways you can build the joy of the Lord in your life.

5. What role can intentionally giving thanks and singing play?

6. What earthly things bring you little joys? Plan to do some of those things together soon!

7

HOW TO STAND UP AND FACE YOUR LIONS

Two Nursing Martyrs

Courage is fear that has said its prayers
-Dorothy Bernard

This chapter presents another facet of the same prism reflecting the power to live UP but is *expressly* about learning how to access the elixir of courage in times of specific crisis. By now, it is manifest that living UP is not found in taking the easy road. In fact, it requires more character, inner determination, and God-given guts to fulfill His purpose than it does to float downstream with the rest of humanity. It takes a higher vision, a greater purpose and an eternal perspective on life to keep moving upward through challenges and pain.

Moms who are reading this next true story from Roman history will be astonished like I was. Becoming a mother altered me forever. I remember how I felt more vulnerable and vicious in the weeks just after giving birth than at any other time. My emotions were acutely intensified as my hormones were radically roller-coasting. Fierce maternal instincts to love and protect my child were alarmingly forceful, emerging seemingly out of "nowhere" as soon as I delivered. I understood the phrase, "Don't mess with a mother bear," with full clarity. So did my husband while observing my extreme emotional swings.

Having experienced an instant and intense desire to protect my newly born children, this story of two young, nursing mothers from Roman history captivates me. To me, they are the most revered examples of believers taking courage in a life or death crisis. One of noble birth and another a slave, these young ladies bravely died as Christian martyrs in Carthage, North Africa, on March 7, 203. Perpetua was only twenty-two, a wife and the mother of a nursing baby boy. Felicitas was also a young woman who had just given birth to a daughter *two* days before her scheduled execution.

While in prison awaiting execution in the arena, Perpetua's wealthy, pagan, and *very* anxious father came to visit several times, carrying her newborn baby, *pleading* with her to offer the sacrifice to Caesar of a few grains of incense to save her life and the life of her dependent, fragile son. Perpetua recorded these incidents and historians have validated their authenticity. The following is one conversation she had with her desperate father, revealing her remarkable courage and faith.

"'Daughter,' he said, 'have pity on my gray hairs; have pity on thy father. Do not give me over to disgrace. Behold thy brothers, thy mother, and thy aunt: behold thy child who cannot live without thee. Do not destroy us all.' Thus spake my father, kissing my hands, and throwing himself at my feet. And I wept because of my father, for he alone of all my family would not rejoice in my martyrdom. So I comforted him, saying:

'In this trial what God determines will take place. We are not in our own keeping but in God's.' So he left me – weeping bitterly."

Eyewitnesses recorded the following description of their entrance into eternity before the raving, bloodthirsty crowd in the Roman arena.

"Perpetua and another Christian woman, Felicitas, were tossed and gored by a bull; but despite cruel manglings, yet survived."

"Perpetua," says a sympathizing recorder, "seemed in a trance."

'When are we to be tossed?' she asked, and could scarcely be induced to believe that she had suffered, in spite of the marks on her body. They were presently stabbed to death by gladiators after having exhorted the others to 'stand fast in the faith and love one another,' she guided to her own throat the uncertain hand of the young gladiator." [1]

If They Could Stand...So Can You

Envisioning this display of sacrificial faith brings tears to my eyes. Facing this excruciating test at *any* time of life would be frightening enough. But these two heroines faced this temptation with fresh milk leaking from their breasts, knowing that their stand would cost not only their own lives but most likely the lives of their tender, infant children. They tapped into a source of strength and courage that few have known. I am speechless as I meditate on their dedication and supernatural courage. I hope someday to talk personally to Perpetua and Felicitas

1. "Death of a Martyr, 203 AD" EyeWitness to History, www.eyewitnesstohistory.com (2004).

when we meet in eternity. I will tell them how much they motivated and inspired me to press on.

There are multitudes of such stories of Christian men, women, and children who praised God boldly while being thrown to ferocious lions and wild beasts. Where did they get such courage? History records that many of the astonished onlookers of these spectacles became believers by the witness of these bold Christians who faced a gruesome death with peace and a song on their lips.

This "taking of courage" is something each of us must learn to do. If martyrs can take courage facing death, we can surely face our less sensational but equally frightening "lions" with His courage.

Courage for Us Today

There have been more Christian martyrs in recent years than all the previous years of persecution combined. [2] Believers of all ages are boldly laying down their lives for the testimony of the gospel around the world even as I write and you read. Their visible joy and courage in both Roman and contemporary days underscore the reality of a supernatural source of "encouragement" that we can experience *no matter* how perilous the challenge may be before us. This courage they expressed allowed them to finish their race victoriously. It

2. http://www.gordonconwell.edu/resources/documents/csgc_Christian_martyrs.pdf

came from above, was deposited inside of them by the Spirit of God, and is still available to those of us who want to finish our races faithfully and give honor to Christ today. Without this supernatural infusion, we will stop short of reaching our high calling.

There is a higher plane we can live in that supersedes the particular set of circumstantial cards we've been dealt. There is a source available to us that issues from heaven to complete the assignments He gives. This "taking of courage" is something each of us must *learn* to do. If martyrs can take courage facing death, we can surely face our less sensational but equally frightening renditions of "lions" with His courage. The same mighty God is *our* fortress. This story illustrates a time when God gave me the courage to jump a much smaller but still looming hurdle of fear in my own life.

Moving to Israel? I Was Terrified! Missing a Bomb by 10 Minutes

Courage: The capacity to go ahead in spite of fear.
-Scott Peck

I sat horrified, looking at the images of bloody, slain bodies of American tourists lying on a familiar Jerusalem street.

These images dominated the evening news. Even in the early '80s, innocent tourists were murdered... just for being Americans and visiting Jerusalem. Terror attacks like these were on the increase in Israel, effectively deterring tourism which is so vital to the economy.

I breathed in deeply and exhaled, "And that is the *exact* street I will be walking on in a few weeks with my blonde-haired three and five-year-old son and daughter!" Fear strangled my next breath..."Maybe I *should* leave them at home with grandma," I pondered. Her recent pleas echoed in my head, "It's one thing to expose *yourself* to such danger, but don't do it to my little grandchildren!"

Bruce and I had been called to Israel for projects several times before as husband and wife. The danger and risk made it all the more exciting...then. This time we were going for months so that Bruce could go to Hebrew school and we were bringing our innocent young children. I knew it was an important commitment and knew better than to resist a God assignment because of danger, but was inwardly in *great* turmoil.

My maternal instincts were screaming that this was *way over* the edge of wisdom. How would I feel if my precious Naomi or Jesse were hurt, taken hostage or, God forbid, shot down in the market streets like those on the news? Why was it so hard to push through this tormenting fear?

I desperately needed some of that "Spirit-infused, heart-strength to venture forward."

I searched for truth in the scriptures. I fastidiously studied, memorized, and quoted out loud protection verses from Psalm 91: "*No* evil will befall you, neither shall *any* plague come near your dwelling, they shall fall at your right hand and at your left, but it *will not* come near you..." Still, the emotional storm raged inside me. Images of the murdered tourists projected before me as I closed my eyes to try to sleep.

I knew better than to be stopped by fear and determined that no matter *how I felt*, I would follow His directive and trust Him. We continued making our plans to go...but inwardly I was crying out for help. "God, I need *fresh* courage to complete this assignment. Past grace is gone; I need new power for this assignment right now."

About a week before our departure date, the help from heaven arrived. Just as I was about to drift off to sleep, I sensed a warm and comforting presence in the room. Someone was standing next to my side of our queen-sized bed. It was Jesus. I couldn't see Him in the dark but felt Him standing there, as real as if it was my husband. Jesus leaned over, lifted my upper body, pressed my head to His chest, and held me, silently.

A tangible and unearthly peace enveloped and filled me

like the steam from a hot aromatherapy shower. Time stood still. He gently laid me back down upon my pillow, and I was aware that I was somehow transformed. His courage had entered and *completely extinguished* the tormenting fear I had daily battled for months. It vanished at last. In that sacred moment, these words floated through my mind, "You take care of what's precious to Me, and I will take care of what's precious to you." The Living Word had spoken and my heart understood. I was willing to go even full of fear to complete this assignment in obedience, but He was gracious enough to meet me with the luxury of this visitation to impart a *fresh* supply of courage for this mother's trembling heart. I can only imagine a similar but even greater impartation of courage that came just at the right time to Perpetual and Felicitas. He is truly the same yesterday, today, and forever.

From that second on, I had perfect tranquility traveling to and then living in West Jerusalem with my precious, little children. There was a lively, outdoor market I loved to walk to through the Dung Gate of the Old City. The air was full of eastern spices as the vendors spread out their piles of vegetables, fruits, spices, brass trinkets, olive wood, carved icons, and brightly hued, woven blankets all over the ground. Naomi and Jesse were trained to cling tightly to me as we wandered these aisles, enjoying this colorful scene heightened by the boisterous bargaining shouts in Arabic and the constant horns honking of outside traffic. One morning, just minutes after we had just skipped through this ancient market to buy sweet Jaffa oranges and gooey baklava, we heard the blast of a bomb that blew up at the gate entrance we had *just minutes before* slipped through. My heart was beating wildly as I realized how His supernatural protection had delivered us from death. "It shall not come near you," I remembered with assurance.

Jesus imparted courage, "the heart-strength to venture, resist opposition and fulfill our assignment" that pivotal night before leaving, and grace sufficient for the journey. Although we were prayerful and alert, I never felt more secure in His care. We took care of what was precious to Him, and as He promised, He took care of what was precious to us.

BONUS BOOSTER

In the mind of God, you have already been released from the power of darkness and sin has no more power to dominate you.

"For we know that our old self was crucified with him so that the body ruled by sin might be done away with,

that we should no longer be slaves to sin because anyone who has died has been set free from sin," Romans 6:7

Sinners are not sitting at the right hand of God in Christ. Sons and daughters made holy by the blood of Jesus are!

He has already paid for your ticket to sit with Him next to the Majesty on High.

Small-Group Discussion – Journal Reflections

SIX: STAND UP AND FACE YOUR LIONS

Answer with a friend, a group, or individually in a journal.

1. What were your reactions to the story of the two young mothers' faith and martyrdom?

2. Why is taking courage a command, versus a suggestion to us?

3. Review and discuss the meaning of the word encouragement and why we need it.

"Holy Spirit infused "encouragement" boosts us with heart-strength to venture, persevere, and resist opposition in order to fulfill our divine purpose and see concrete results.

4. Share an experience of taking courage from your own life.

5. Pray about how you can apply this to your life right now?

8

HOW DID JOSHUA STAND UP?

A champion is someone who gets up when he can't.
-Jack Dempsey

Every great accomplishment on earth directed by the Spirit of God requires that we learn *how* to draw from Him the courage necessary to fulfill it. This in-depth Bible study will reveal more insight into this. Moses needed the burning-bush encounter, Deborah needed the commission under the palm tree to "march," Mary needed the visitation and promise of the angel Gabriel, Joseph needed the dream, Esther needed the revelation that she had come to power "for such a time as this," and Gideon required his fleece. What do all these heroes have in common? Strength springing from the living word of God. We are blessed to have the written word of God to encourage us. His Word contains *living courage* to act.

How you *face* the inevitable lions or giants as you journey into *your* promised land will determine the outcome. Count on it, you *will* face them. Jesus promised, "These things I have spoken to you, so that in Me you may have peace. In the world, you *will have tribulation*, but *take courage*; I have overcome the world," John 16:33. But you can confront them in a new and positive way. Instead of letting obstacles devour or deter you, you can *rise up* in the midst of them stronger and better, and *take courage* from the Commander of your destiny.

Several times the Bible mentions this vital connection between receiving courage in order to be energized to take important steps of action, whether large or seemingly small. Check out this partial list of a variety of difficult situations mentioned, noting the specific command to and the corresponding result of "taking courage".

Every great accomplishment on earth directed by the Spirit of God requires that we learn how to draw from Him the courage necessary to fulfill it.

Joseph of Arimathea: "Joseph of Arimathea came, a prominent member of the Council, who himself was waiting for the kingdom of God; and *he gathered up courage* and went in before Pilate, and asked for the body of Jesus." Mark 15:43

Solomon: "Consider now, for the LORD has chosen you to build a house for the sanctuary; *be courageous and act.*" 1 Chronicles 28:10

Shekaniah to Ezra: "Arise! For this matter is your responsibility, but we will be with you; *be courageous and act.*" Ezra 10:4

Joab and the armies of Israel before battle: "Be strong, and *let us show ourselves courageous f*or the sake of our people and for the cities of our God; and may the LORD do what is good in His sight." 1 Chronicles 19:13

Asa: "But you, be strong and *do not lose courage*, for there is a reward for your work." Now when Asa heard these words and the prophecy which Azariah the son of Oded the prophet spoke, *he took courage* and removed the abominable idols from all the land of Judah and Benjamin and from the cities which he had captured in the hill country of Ephraim. He then restored the altar of the LORD which was in front of the porch of the LORD. 2 Chronicles 15:7-8

God to Joshua: "*Be strong and courageous*, for you shall give this people possession of the land which I swore to their fathers to give them.

Be strong and very courageous. Be careful to obey all the law my servant Moses gave you; do not turn from it to the right or to the left, that you may be successful wherever you go. Keep this Book of the Law always on your lips; meditate on it day and night, so that you may be careful to do everything written in it. *Then* you will be prosperous and successful. Have I not commanded you? *Be strong and courageous.* Do not be afraid; do not be discouraged, for the Lord your God will be with you wherever you go." Joshua 1:6-9

Your life will be no different; you will need to be strong and courageous to carry out His commission.

A deeper study of Joshua's life is an outstanding demonstration of this truth. While exploring his life challenges and assignment, I pondered this passage describing God's motivational speech to him to "take courage." Joshua, the personal disciple, understudy, and servant of Moses for many years, was entering a *very* critical mission from God. He had witnessed all the incredible leadership challenges and mighty miracles that God performed through the mighty Moses. The plagues of Egypt leading to the grand exodus of Israel from bondage, the literal parting of the Red Sea, daily manna to eat falling from heaven, and water spewing out of rock were just *a few* of these amazing manifestations. Now God was calling Joshua up to bat to take Moses' place of leadership. The stage was set, and the audience was waiting. Talk about an intimidating act to follow. His proverbial knees were shaking.

Joshua was clearly chosen by God to succeed Moses' after his death. It was *his* turn to step up to the plate of destiny and offer himself. Can you relate to the feelings of self-doubt with which Joshua must have struggled? How could he *ever* come close to filling Moses' shoes and lead the people into the Promised Land if Moses couldn't? Who would ever follow *him*? The mission no doubt seemed overwhelming, impossible, and mind-boggling. I would guess that you have felt similar apprehension and fear when looking at your assignments and the myriad obstacles before you? We will revisit Joshua after this story of my first somewhat formidable overseas missions trip.

Thrust Into Ministry in Taiwan

I was nervous when taking my first overseas missions trip to Taiwan. I felt waves of insecurity and doubt. I was the youngest of a team of thirty others, most of whom were seasoned pastors. I was a single, brand-new, high school teacher. We were traveling to assist a well-known Chinese evangelist to hold large stadium evangelistic crusades. I didn't know *anyone* but reminded myself of how I had felt a direct push from the Lord to join this outreach. I repeated this prayer of commitment quietly as our plane was about to land in Taiwan, "So here I am, Lord, send me."

The humidity and heat in Taiwan in August were sweltering, a hundred times worse than in Missouri in summer. Jet lag and excitement about our bus ride to the arena awakened me far earlier than necessary the next day.

Waiting for the hot sun to rise, I laid quietly in bed, praying, "I've always wanted to minister in Asia, Lord." I recalled how ecstatic I was when I opened the confirming check which was slipped into my hand at my last mid-week home group...$2,000.00! "Thank You so much for miraculously supplying for me to come here, and please let me touch the people with your love."

Eager and first on the bus, I marveled at the sunrise revealing a world of contrasts. Fascinating scenes of emerald, terraced, rice paddies, rickshaws, and roaming water buffalos juxtaposed next to tall skyscrapers and glitzy department stores. An aged, blind woman, dressed in rags, was fanning herself with a silk embroidered fan, begging for coins. She sat on the same corner where men in three-piece navy business suits rushed by quickly.

Children dressed in British-looking blue uniforms walked double-file into their schools next to an alley where turbaned, tribal women spread out their turnips and tomatoes on the ground to sell. I noted this east meets west paradox. Instantly, I felt a deep connection with these beautiful and meek Asian people, drawn to their tangible sense of humility and grace.

Stunned and excited by the sight as I entered the massive stadium. A crowd of 30,000 people already *filled* already the massive, circular building. I calmed myself. These multitudes had come from all around the nation and were waiting patiently to hear the good news of Jesus Christ. I sat with our group in the stands, wiping sheets of sweat from my brow and feeling out of place as the least experienced. I glanced behind me one row, and I thought I saw what looked like a giant, green serpent. I did a double-take. This long, green, three-inch-wide snake was tattooed on several bodies, starting from their faces, wrapping around their necks, and extending all the way to their toes. I inhaled and exhaled slowly for a moment and then couldn't resist looking again. This time I tried to look beyond the dragon and into their eyes to smile at them. Most had black or missing teeth, but I didn't notice that as much as the warm return of giggles and loving smiles. These grins reached across the centuries of an incredible cultural gulf between us, to mysteriously connect our hearts. I tried unobtrusively to inquire of our guide about this intriguing right-out-of-a-National-Geographic-magazine group sitting behind us.

"These people come from a tribe of mountain people, some of whom have come to know Jesus. They are from a clan of animists, who worship the tree and snake spirits." The six-foot emerald tattoos winding around their bodies confirmed that he was telling the truth. "These believers love Jesus so much that they have literally walked *for weeks* to get here," he explained, as my jaw dropped automatically in disbelief. I contrasted this zeal with my own and felt...honored just to be in their presence. My eyes glimpsed their weathered, sandaled feet in amazement. "What excuses have I ever used about why I couldn't attend a gathering?" I compared introspectively. I wished that I could speak their language to learn more from them. But the sight of their blistered feet spoke unforgettable volumes.

Suddenly, the high-pitched melodies of Chinese voices reverberated throughout the stadium. The masses began to clap and sway. The atmosphere was electric. I was just a little, white speck in a sea of Asian faces. The children, in particular, captured my eyes and heart. Their thick, black, shiny hair, cut bluntly around their neck, perfectly framed their moon-shaped, fair faces. These little dolls would shyly giggle and slightly bow every time we made eye contact. I wanted to take all of them home with me. What impressed me most is that they wholeheartedly burst out in singing, not the least bit bashful, praising at the top of their lungs. This was the seed planted in my heart for later adopting our daughter Hannah, from China.

The Chinese evangelist delivered a passionate message of her conversion from communism to Christ in spite of torture and persecution. Surviving an attempted execution by a gun squad, her story captivated these thousands, many openly weeping, for a solid hour. I was so immersed in this "other-time and other-place" experience, that I never wanted it to end.

Unprepared for what happened next, the speaker prayed for those who wanted to receive Christ and then boldly announced that God wanted to heal the sick people attending and for her American team to come to the front to pray for them. That meant me! I was jolted out of my reverie. I had never been called on to do anything like that before. I panicked on the inside, no doubt feeling a little of what Joshua felt trying to step into Moses' shoes.

She beckoned the team to come forward to stand around the platform in front in order to pray for the stampeding mass of people streaming toward us. The blind, crippled, deaf, diseased, wheel-chaired, bruised masses of humanity, old and young, including the tribal groups, pushed ahead for prayer like an undulating serpent. Overcome with compassion for them, I was forced to quickly get my eyes *off of myself*, my inexperience, my inadequacy, and intimidation and put them squarely on the Lord.

"Jesus, Your Word says that You are the same, yesterday, today, and forever. So please heal the individuals in these masses through me, whom You know by name. Touch these people through my hands and I will be your gloves," I pleaded. In a way, I was calling for Him to "infuse me with heart-strength to venture, not turn away and fulfill His purpose for me" that moment. Before I knew it, people were pressing all around me, pointing to places on their bodies that needed healing. I simply gently touched them and prayed simple prayers. Jesus did the rest. To my amazement, they were receiving immediate relief and began to cry out and praise God in their native tongue in thanksgiving. We were all crying and hugging. Never so touched in all my life by the sincere faith and hunger of these precious God-seekers, I felt humbled to be the "available mud" God had moved into position and used to touch their lives. I thanked God that I was given no time to worry, try to escape, argue, or remember that I was under-trained. The crowd was upon me and so was the Holy Spirit. I had to spontaneously *take courage,* act, and let Him show off His power. The next morning I was told I would be leading the worship for the children's crusade of many thousands. Really? No time to argue that I wasn't prepared, I just said, "Okay," and had the time of my life leading those angelic, Asian voices in unforgettable melodies of heavenly praise. God poured in the courage and His glory followed effortlessly.

"Stand Up, Joshua"

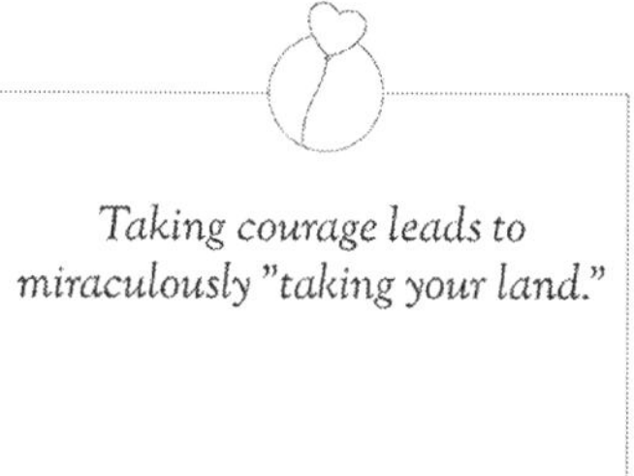

Taking courage leads to miraculously "taking your land."

God treated Joshua's inner intimidation just like He did mine. Rather than comfort him with sweet words of empathy and coaxing, He simply gave him a direct commission and promise in an authoritative command:

"Be strong and courageous, for you shall give this people possession of the land." "Only be strong and courageous. Have I not commanded you? Be strong and courageous. Do not tremble or be dismayed, for the Lord Your God is with you wherever you go." Joshua 1: 6, 7, 9, & 18.

No slack here. No time for a pity party, for a prayer meeting, or an explanation of his deficiencies or inexperience. He simply commanded him *several times* to be strong and courageous, period. No talking back or asking questions now. Just a direct command to obey: be strong and courageous. The promise was that He would do the rest. "And I will..."

In Deuteronomy 3:28, God had previously instructed Moses to purposefully encourage and strengthen Joshua in preparation for his future role in leading Israel through the promised land. He would absolutely *need supernatural courage* to fulfill his assignment.

"But charge Joshua and *encourage him and strengthen him*; for he shall go across at the head of this people, and he shall give them as an inheritance the land which you will see." This progression repeats over and over so we can "get it."

The Spirit of God knew that for Joshua to lead the people through the many obstacles and intense battles ahead, he would absolutely need to depend on the power of God, the word of God, and the strength of God to get the job done. It wasn't about him, anyway. Responding to this command to be strong and courageous was crucial, momentous, and foundational to all Joshua would be called to do. Taking courage leads to miraculously "taking your land."

Here is a helpful secret to know about every command you see in the scriptures. With *every* command in the scriptures comes the provision to obey it. You are commanded to love one another as Christ has loved you because He has filled you with the power to do so. Apart from Him, you can do *nothing*. But because you abide in Him and He abides in you, you can do *all things* He commands, by His very own power-supply flowing through you. Your being courageous comes *only* from this vital abiding in Him. God's courage resides inside of you because Christ resides there. He activates it as you depend on Him. You don't have to feel His love or courage first...you must act on it by faith. I learned that in Taiwan. Without faith, it is *impossible* to please God. But with it, it is impossible *not* to please him. Do not wait to *feel* bold or courageous, or you will miss out on *so* many miracles.

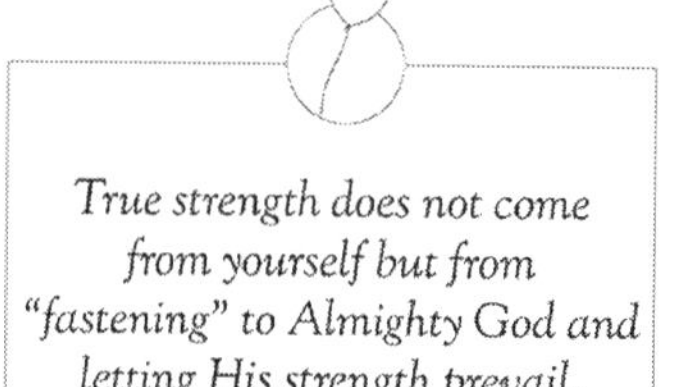

True strength does not come from yourself but from "fastening" to Almighty God and letting His strength prevail.

The meaning of "strong" and "courageous" gives great insight. Part of the definition of "strong" means "to fasten to and prevail." True strength does not come from yourself but from "fastening" to Almighty God and letting His strength prevail. "Courage" means "inner heart-strength to venture, persevere and resist opposition, empowerment to achieve one's ends, to be steadfast minded, fearless and unyielding." To be strong and courageous literally means to fasten yourself to God steadfastly and watch Him prevail *through* you. I love that. It's not that I tough it out with whatever measly stamina I can muster up to endure the storm. No, I fall completely into His arms, fastening all my hope and faith in His ability and simply allow Him to show off his power in my weakness. That is what those Christians in the Coliseum understood. They fastened themselves to His strength and let His courage prevail through them to astound the world.

The new testament unveils this amazing opportunity for you to experience His strength in a similar command found in Ephesians 6:10:

"Finally, brethren, be strong in the Lord and in the strength of *His* might." Remember that the command *carries with it* the supernatural ability to do it!

The Lord also orders Joshua (and you) to not be *dismayed.* This mandate is another key to avoiding discouragement. "Dismayed" means" to "look around in amazement, to be bewildered, to look away and inspect." If the believers in the Roman arenas had focused on the size and teeth of the lions, or the tenderness of their child's flesh, fear would have overtaken them. They would have trembled and screamed. It is the same for you as you face any kind of problem. You can look away from the reality of Christ inside of you and focus on the problem until you feel overtaken. Or you can focus your thoughts unwaveringly on the Lord and allow Him to empower you. You can cling to His strength inside of you. Whatever you dwell on will grow larger in your assessment of things. Joshua passed on this same command to the Israelites when they were facing the dreadful battles conquering the land from their reputed invincible enemies.

"And Joshua said unto them, Fear not, nor be dismayed, be strong and of good courage: for thus shall the LORD do to all your enemies against whom ye fight." Joshua 10:25, KJV

The meaning of the word "discouraged" is interestingly "to liquefy or melt," "to collapse," and "to break down by confusion, fatigue or fear."

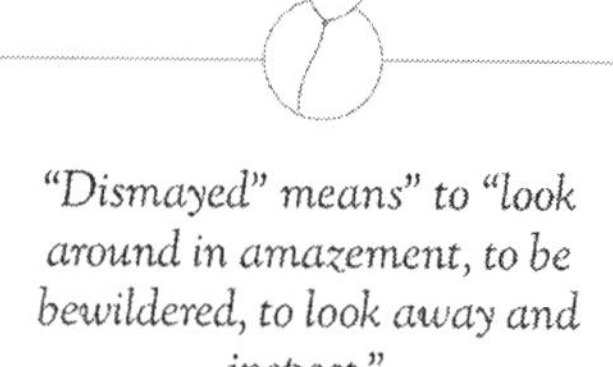

"Dismayed" means" to "look around in amazement, to be bewildered, to look away and inspect."

The pattern is clear. If you concentrate on the complications, disappointments, and problems that confront you or on your own inadequacies, your dismay becomes discouragement and you will begin to collapse or "melt" on the inside. That is what happened to me as I kept my view on the TV images of the slaughtered tourists in Jerusalem. Instead of prevailing and overcoming, I began to faint and melt with fear.

The two options are crystal clear. You will either *prevail* by fastening to the Lord and watching Him do the works, or you will *melt* and give in if you center your attention on yourself and the obstacles. My encounter with the Fearless One allowed my heart to literally take courage for the assignment...in order to complete it fully and give Him glory.

Joshua, like the "heroes" before him, also procured courage and strength from the Lord and completed his destiny to bring the children of Israel into their promised land. At the end of his life, this is a worthy tribute made to him about his life:

"Now it came about after many days when the LORD had given rest to Israel from all their enemies on every side, and Joshua was old, advanced in years..." Joshua 23:1.

That is *quite* a statement of success and victory. Through the courage of Joshua supplied by the God of Israel, passed on to the people of Israel, they had *fully* taken their inherited land. *All* the foreign enemies were defeated and a major mission was accomplished. Joshua did seize miraculous courage and as a result, gave the people possession of their God-given land. Not only that but under his leadership and as a result of his example something more awesome took place: the people served the Lord.

"Then Joshua dismissed the people, each to his inheritance. And it came about after these things that Joshua the son of Nun, the servant of the LORD, died, being one hundred and ten years old. And they buried him in the territory of his inheritance in Timnath-serah, which is in the hill country of Ephraim, on the north of Mount Gaash. And Israel served the LORD all the days of Joshua and all the days of the elders who survived Joshua and had known all the deeds of the LORD which He had done for Israel, Joshua 24:28-31.

I can think of no higher honor and legacy that could be attributed to him.

Application: So *Let* Your Heart Take Courage

Joshua had learned the secret of living "not by might, nor by power, but by My Spirit, says the Lord" found in Zechariah 4:6. That is *exactly* how you can run and complete your race today. David refers to this crucial exchange as "letting your heart take courage" when he writes from experience in Psalm 27:13-14: "I would have despaired *unless* I had believed that I would see the goodness of the Lord in the land of the living. Wait for the Lord; be strong and *let* your heart take courage. Yes, wait for the Lord." And again in Psalm 31:24, he repeats this exhortation: "Be strong and *let* your heart take courage, all you who hope in the Lord." This spiritual nugget excites me. My heart, (the root part, "cour" of the word "courage" means heart) can "take in" divine empowerment any time if I "let" it. These verses underscore the importance of *opening* our hearts to courage. It also implies that there are times that you may forget and wallow and whine and not "let" your heart take courage.

The good news is that we don't have to stay there, stuck emotionally. You can possess your own "promised land," like Joshua, by being strong (fastening to the Lord) and authorizing your heart to "take courage." Do not tremble and be dismayed, looking at the difficulties before you rather than at God's *unlimited* resources inside you *ready* to prevail.

God's command to *take* courage is inspiring. If the whole world and all your friends are not giving you encouragement, you have a higher source of courage. You can *take* courage, as much as you need and more, from the One who is with you "wherever you may go."

Staying discouraged is not an option if you want to fulfill your call and express your divine story. Discouragement is designed to abort your dreams and get you to melt under the heat and pressure of the fight. Even if no one is around to encourage you, the Greater One inside of you is *ready* to strengthen, empower and carry you through to a victorious conclusion. Joshua looked to Him, and sure enough, battle after battle, God kept His word and gave the people their inheritance. And unlike Joshua and the many other leaders in the Bible before the time of Christ who were commanded to take courage, you live under the new covenant wherein God's Spirit lives *inside* of you. You are already filled with the power of His might. Be strong and courageous!

May our Lord Jesus Christ Himself and God our Father,
who loved us and by His grace,
gave us eternal encouragement and good hope,

encourage your hearts and strengthen you
in every good deed and word.
2 Thessalonians 2:16-17.

Taking Courage to Cross the Border into a Communist Country

Knowing and practicing this truth allowed me to complete another important task given to me years after my trip to Taiwan... to take Bibles to the underground church in the Far East.

The irritated passport official frowned as he pointed out an error on my entrance card. My shoulders tightened with the pressure of the moment. I clumsily entered the right information and after another scowl, was dismissed to the next guard.

"Help me not to blow this, God, because these Bibles need to get to your suffering people here," I prayed as if He needed to be reminded. I remembered why I was doing this. Our team had begged, borrowed, fasted, prayed, and thrown ourselves into this mission to bring the precious word of life to these believers. Despite severe persecution at this time, the secret house-church movement had flourished to many millions of passionate believers with thousands of people being born again every day. When asked how the west might help to stop the torture and persecution, many sufferers reply, "Don't pray that persecution will stop. Persecution is *good* for the spreading of the gospel! No, pray that we will continue to love and forgive our torturers and show them the love of Christ." I wanted to help believers with that *rare* kind of dedication and zeal.

I nervously recalled my instructions. "After they inspect your passport, proceed. Ignore the "scan all bags here" sign. Do not have eye contact with any guards. Fiddle with your passport and if anyone calls to you, act like you don't hear him. Unless a guard physically restrains you, just keep walking." "Just keep walking," I rehearsed to myself as my heart was pounding like drums at a rock concert.

"Just keep walking" I repeated to myself over and over as I passed each uniformed guard and potential stopping place, anxious about being stopped. I determined not to let fear have the last word. I was consciously taking courage from the Lord. How inane that I had to hide, not illegal drugs or laundered black market money, but copies of the Bible inside my bags. I imagined groups of believers huddled in a secret gathering praying for the honor of someday touching, let alone possessing this banned, love letter from heaven. My thoughts drifted to those who at that very moment were enduring torture in prison cells for simply being caught with one. I wanted to serve these true believers... so unlike the many flavors of "chocolate soldiers" so common in my country, so pampered and consumed with living comfortably and melting down with the slightest bit of adversity.

Twenty excruciatingly long and unhindered steps past the last guard, an incredible rush of relief came with the realization that I had completed a safe crossing. An adrenaline high better than a Starbucks double espresso shot kicked in. It only increased as I realized that one by one, each courier from our team successfully repeated the same triumph in this drama. Standing at our meeting place, a knowing look passed between us that implied our mutual but hidden elation. Grins of satisfaction became visible as we got further away from scrutiny.

Thinking about how grateful the recipients of these gifts would give me a thoughtful pause. Each Bible would impact at least ten people in the underground church. Even though they risked imprisonment and torture for receiving them, they were not deterred. Stories of their bravery and sacrifice to live out their faith no matter the cost captured my heart. Women younger than me were arrested and beaten for sharing Christ with children. Their humble homes were being bulldozed down as a punishment for hosting a prayer gathering.

What an inexpressible feeling of honor to be able to be a small part in touching the lives of these hidden heroes.

We deposited our treasure in a secret place for a future pick up by these known *only to God's* daring disciples. A warmth of deep gladness welled up inside, knowing that I would see their faces...somewhere beyond this earthly life, in a place where suffering and injustice would be no more. His courage was passed on through us to those who would doubly need it.

What assignment is brewing around in your heart that you know you are to complete... but have felt intimidated by its size or difficulty? Has fear kept you from understanding how to "let your heart take courage"? I pray that this chapter would be a catalyst to spark your hope and excitement that *you can do it* by fastening to Him and taking courage. May He energize and encourage you *this very moment* to take the next step.

Remember, Jesus Himself warned that you would have intense challenges while living upon this fallen planet. But He gave us a statement, a promise, and an instruction that echoes and summarizes everything about the absolute necessity, the life-giving transfusion of "taking courage" in our lives. "These things I have spoken to you, that in Me you may have peace. In the world, you will have tribulation, *but take courage*; I have overcome the world," John 16:33.

Find out in the next few chapters how David, as a type of Christ and Jesus Himself would apply His own advice.

BONUS BOOSTER

You can live NOW in the newness of resurrection life in Christ.

We were therefore buried with him through baptism into death in order that,

just as Christ was raised from the dead through the glory of the Father, we too may live a new life. Romans 6:4

His word says we can "put off your old self which belongs to your former manner of life, and put on the new self,

created after the likeness of God in true righteousness and holiness," Ephesians 4:22-24

Simply CHANGE CLOTHES! Put off the old and put on and live in the new. Conduct your activities and choices as you would sitting right next to Jesus on high.

Small-Group Discussion – Journal Reflections

SEVEN: HOW DID JOSHUA STAND UP?

1. Discuss why God commanded Joshua to be strong and courageous.

2. Share when you felt completely inadequate for a task. What happened?

3. What did you learn about being dismayed or discouraged and how to combat both?

4. Explore the phrase "let your heart take courage." What is our part in obeying this?

5. Try to identify what keeps you from doing this?

6. Pray about how you can apply this to your life right now?

9

HOW TO CHEER UP EVEN WHEN YOU'RE ALL ALONE

Encouraging Yourself in the Lord

When others let you down, look up.
-Anonymous

And David was greatly distressed;
for the people spake of stoning him,
because the soul of all the people was grieved,
every man for his sons and for his daughters:
but David encouraged himself in the LORD his God.
1 Samuel 30:6

There will be times when *no one* on earth will be there to strengthen us. Some of us may already know that all too well. The beautiful good news is that there is One who is always with us, will *never* forsake us, and thoroughly understands.

The purpose of this chapter is to reveal that *the art of encouraging yourself*, strange as it may sound, is actually an invigorating and life-saving skill *we can learn*. I never took a college class or read a book about this lost practice, but gleaned it from the Bible and the school of hard knocks. I pass on these secrets, using two people from the Bible: David, and Jesus.

David exemplified graduate-level mastery in this mostly unknown practice. And most of all, Jesus supremely exhibits this for us on the cross.

David was on the run. A new national hit song was being sung by the people in Israel, enraging King Saul: "Saul has slain his thousands, but David his *tens* of thousands." Murderously jealous, Saul was seeking David's death.

The prophet Samuel had openly anointed David to be the next king, but David had many years to pass an important character test: to wait for the Lord to raise him up in *His* time rather than take matters into his own hands. Although David had several chances to kill Saul during this life chapter of waiting, and many of his men counseled him to do just that, David would not lift his hand up to touch the "Lord's anointed." The price to pay for this display of integrity, for doing the *right* thing, was that he lived in disgrace as a fugitive in exile for years. This reminds me of Joseph's years in prison for *not* committing adultery. God prepares our character to match our assignments and the trials that often produce this character are rarely what we would describe as enjoyable.

I love that although it was clearly God's plan to make him king, David was not willing to take immoral shortcuts or promote himself. He wanted God's plan and God's timing. Rare leadership qualities for sure.

God Sends Friends

God was faithful to send strength to David during this extremely difficult period in his life. He used David's best friend, Jonathan, the son of Saul, to uphold and refresh him. David and Jonathan developed a friendship centered on God that was like none other and, no doubt was divinely created to supply essential courage to each other. Their relationship became a rich supply of joy and reinforcement they both would need in order to carry out the critical quests they were facing. The Author of friendship gives us those "once-in-a-lifetime" and "for such a time as this" companions with whom we can supernaturally connect and support. The following verses capture a look at the intensity and importance of David and Jonathan's brotherly bond of love.

The soul of Jonathan was knit to the soul of David, and Jonathan loved him as himself, 1 Samuel 18:1. *And Jonathan made David vow again because of his love for him because he loved him as he loved his own life,* 1 Samuel 20:17.

Jonathan learned of his father's plan to kill David and providentially warned him to flee. He would also visit David in hiding and continually uplift and embolden David for the purposes of God. There is nothing as inestimable in value as a God-sent ally who stands with you in your times of testing and aloneness...nothing.

Now David became aware that Saul had come out to seek his life while David was in the wilderness of Ziph at Horesh. And Jonathan, Saul's son, arose and went to David at Horesh, and encouraged him in God, I Samuel 23:16.

This exemplifies the highest role a true friend can play in our lives: to pay whatever the cost to stand with us and see the plan of God carried out in our lives. Jonathan faithfully stood with David in his infamous times of humiliation and shame, in his times of testing, and in his times of insignificance. He never lived to enjoy the days of David's glory as King. But without the supporting devotion of Jonathan, perhaps David might have lacked the strength he needed to endure the painful suffering of injustice and rejection. Our Father beneficently uses chosen friends to uphold us at strategic times in our journey. These vessels are His visible hands extended to us. We can be that kind of spiritual friend to key people in our life.

From Dung to Diamonds

I get by with a little help from my friends.
The Beatles

I froze in my tracks, dropping the jar of baby applesauce I held.

Familiar women's voices from my church arrested my attention, floating over from the next grocery aisle.

"Don't you love the way our new pastor preaches the Word? He's SOOO sweet to us!"

"Absolutely, I can't WAIT until next week to hear him again!"

My newborn son perched quietly in the blue infant seat in the front of my overflowing grocery cart; the son I would usually rush to show these ladies who had been such a big part of my life. Instead, I wished to disappear. How could I escape without being seen? "I DON'T want them to see me crying, and there is just no way to stop my tears," I resolved to myself. I jerked my tiny baby and his infant seat and ran for the exit, leaving my cart full of the desperately needed newborn diapers and baby food behind.

My sudden dash out the door to the parking lot startled little Jesse who began to wail, making it an impossible struggle to buckle him into the car seat. At the sound of his cries, my engorged breasts released fresh milk that seeped through my blouse.

"Oh, great!" I shrieked, climbing into the back seat. I slammed the door and tried to nurse my disconsolate child while my uncontrollable sobs came in waves. "I can't understand this, God. I've spent the last two and a half years loving those ladies. They were at our home for Thanksgiving, and our kids are best friends; we studied the entire book of James verse by verse together over coffee and bagels.

Not one even came to see me in the hospital last week, when my son was born. How could they abandon me to be a part of this new and "better" group splitting our church family in half? Can't they see what's going on?" My husband and I were very young and inexperienced in pastoring back then and no doubt had made many stupid mistakes. But nothing had prepared me for this awful feeling of rejection and failure. The raging postpartum hormones did not help.

"Oh Jesus," I wrestled within, "These were my closest

girlfriends, my dearest and only support group. I left all my old friends and family behind when coming to plant this church. How could they leave so capriciously after all we've been through?" Fresh hot tears poured out.

Entirely out of tissues, I used my sleeve to wipe my nose and eyes, further staining it. "I feel so betrayed." Gazing at my innocent child, I worried that my grief was so excruciating it was probably making my milk sour. "Oh Jesse," I said, kissing his forehead, "I'm sorry; I don't want you to feel what I'm feeling."

My delicate infant boy had drifted off to sleep after the first breast, so I belted him into his car seat, climbed into the front seat and drove home as a veil of water blurred my vision. Over and over, the thought came to me: "You've got to call your best friend." Still feeling so alone and ashamed, I couldn't bring myself to do it. Just then the phone rang, and it was...her. "I just had you on my heart, girlfriend, how are you?" she inquired.

The words stuck in my throat; her compassionate call drew out more sobbing. I had to call Bruce to the phone to tell her the terrible story of hurt and feelings of betrayal we were experiencing.

"This is unbelievable! I am flying Claudia and the baby home to St. Louis *this* week and we are going to get our friends together and pray," she asserted boldly in her usual "take-action" mode. There was no resisting. This was God's 911 rescue plan for me in this head-on collision, spiritual attack. Emotionally, I was ready for the stretcher, and the spiritual hospital, and my flight was scheduled.

My next vivid memory is of sitting in her French Country navy and sky blue living room, being surrounded by several old friends: singers, preachers, and drama team members, all devoted believers with whom we had a great history together of creating local outreaches, concerts, teams to Israel, and youth events. We had been comrades in arms together for years. I couldn't believe they could drop everything to gather to pray for us. Bruce stayed with our 20-month-old daughter to "hold the fort" and continue ministering.

"You guys are front-line soldiers, no, commanders. Of course, we're going to come and cover your back, here!" one long-haired, fired-up friend declared. "You have laid your lives down to reach the people in your city, and we are going to pray for healing, and a fresh refueling for you to finish the assignment!"

A pile of hands and arms covered me like a down blanket, as I sat Indian style on the blue carpet with Jesse dozing on my lap. Tears rained down my face, as powerful prayer after prayer filled the air for what must have been over an hour. Every need for strength, every feeling of despair, every fear of failure, and every desire of my heart to forgive and move ahead was expressed and put into words by these mediators' prayers. I felt as though all the pain suctioned out of me and new strength infused. It was a supernatural surgery like I had never experienced.

I was the paralyzed man mentioned in Luke 5:19 whose friends wanted to get him to Jesus so severely that they tore open the roof of the room Jesus was in, and lowered their friend on a stretcher down through the hole, right in front of Him. Jesus saw THEIR faith and the man was healed and jumped up off his cot. I was drowning in the lie that I was a miserable failure and should give up. They could see something different.

After the prayers finished, I felt someone putting something on my finger. I opened my eyes to see my dear friend's diamond engagement part of her wedding ring shining on my finger. Opening my mouth to refuse this exorbitant gesture, she immediately hushed me saying, "Wear this as a reminder of how valuable you are, and how precious and eternally significant your ministry is. You've been treated like trash but are truly His royal ambassador."

I was adamantly protesting this gift, wondering what her husband was thinking, and he spoke up, "Wear it, Claudie, and remember who you are every time you look at it!" That was the hardest gift I ever had to receive, but its message continued to give me strength and was a powerful reminder of His encouragement through friends in my life. I later found this confirming scripture:

"You will also be a crown of beauty in the hand of the LORD And a royal diadem in the hand of your God. It will no longer be said to you, "Forsaken," Nor to your land will it any longer be said, "Desolate"; But you will be called, "My delight is in her," And your land, "Married"; For the LORD delights in you, And to Him, your land will be married." Isa. 62: 3-4

This act of love and symbolism undid me. I felt like Moses with his rod, or David with his five smooth stones, ready to go back and face every giant. I do not doubt that my emotional life and future ministry largely was restored by this extreme act of encouragement and extravagant love. A few dedicated believers became a divine gasoline station fueling me with the supernatural courage I needed to keep moving ahead.

About a year later, this beloved couple came to do a multi-media concert in our city. While my beloved friend sang, I knew that I was healed and should return the ring. I walked up to her after the concert with such admiration and love for this friend who had stuck "closer than a brother," handed her the ring, and said, "This ring has done its work in me...may I never doubt my worth again." Decades of ministry assignments were ahead for me, and this vital recharge was one of many along the way. "Encourage the exhausted, and strengthen the feeble. Say to those with anxious heart, "Take courage, fear not." Isaiah 35: 3-4

Defining Moments, Alone

There was another test, however, that David had to face *without* the presence of his dearest comrade in the things of God. In one of David's many adventures while living as a fugitive, a major tragedy occurred described here in 1 Samuel 30: 1-6:

Then it happened when David and his men came to Ziklag on the third day, that the Amalekites had made a raid on the Negev and on Ziklag, and had overthrown Ziklag and burned it with fire; and they took captive the women and all who were in it, both small and great, without killing anyone, and carried them off and went their way. And when David and his men came to the city, behold, it was burned with fire, and their wives and their sons and their daughters had been taken captive. Then David and the people who were with him lifted their voices and wept until there was no strength in them to weep. Now David's two wives had been taken captive, Ahinoam the Jezreelitess and Abigail the widow of Nabal the Carmelite. Moreover, David was greatly distressed because the people spoke of stoning him, for all the people were embittered, each one because of his sons and his daughters.

Imagine their horror returning to their camp and finding it *completely* burned down and all their wives and children kidnapped! Everyone wanted to blame David and even spoke of *stoning* him. Like that would really solve things and bring their families back? People don't often think clearly in the midst of trauma and crisis. It reminds me of the mob mentality Jesus experienced standing before Pilate, when mobs of the same people who one week earlier had joyously waved palm leaves at Him while He rode into Jerusalem shouting," Hosanna, Hosanna," now were screaming, "Crucify Him! Crucify Him!"

> *David knew where to go for encouragement. He went to God Himself. He didn't collapse in self-pity. He ran to the Lord.*

Try to imagine an equivalent scenario as David's in your own life with *so* much responsibility for the lives of so many loved ones on your shoulders. In his shoes, I might have been tempted to flee or tell the men to go ahead and throw those stones and end it all.

The next part of verse 6 is astounding in its content and tells how David responded to this absolute calamity. This is one of the most *important* verses in the Bible about getting through a so-many-lives-depend-on-you crisis. *But David encouraged himself in the LORD his God,* 1 Samuel 30:6.

Incredible. Supernatural. Remarkable. David was *not*

accepting a mediocre ending to his life. Nor was he about to let the name of Yahweh be shamed among the nations. All the supposedly supportive leaders David was training to help him had just lost their wives and kids and were picking up boulders to kill him. Jonathan wasn't anywhere near to come to his defense. But the Lord, His God, stood with him. David knew *where to go* for encouragement. He went to God Himself. He didn't collapse in self-pity. He ran to the Lord.

There are times when there is no prayer chain to call, no mediation team to enlist, no commercial break scheduled, but just *one* place to turn. I believe those alone seasons in our lives are ordained "gifts" to train us to draw solely on our relationship with our faithful Deliverer. Making *Him* our number one source is a key to experiencing just how mighty He is. Knowing Him, becoming familiar with His heart, spending time in His company, and receiving a revelation of His purposes, makes faith almost effortless. It makes believing Him as easy as breathing. That's exactly what David had done to prepare himself for this extreme cliff-hanger emergency.

How did he encourage himself in God? We can discover that by doing a brief study of some of David's many songs. The songs of David recorded in the book of Psalms, expose his rich, heart-to-heart devotional life with the Lord. He is my favorite person/musician/worshiper in the

Bible. He *practiced* receiving strength from God and the intimate relationship he developed *totally* prepared him to move through this supreme test.

David's M.O. in Crisis

A clear pattern unfolds that David had established *years* before to be able to press on through upsetting circumstances. First, he *calls on God*. At the beginning of many of his psalms, he gets right to the point and expresses openly and urgently his need to God. He is not in the least "religious' or pious as we might expect. Listen to these honest cries and spontaneous, bold appeals.

O LORD, I have so many enemies; so many are against me. Psalm 3:1

Answer me when I call, Take away my distress. Psalm 4:1

O LORD, hear me as I pray; pay attention to my groaning. Psalm 5:1

I come to you for protection, O LORD my God. Save me from persecutors–rescue me! Psalm 7:1

I admire how he just lays it all out to the Lord with confidence and expectation that his ever-present God will hear and act on his behalf. The shortest prayer we need to pray is just, "Help!" How refreshing. Practice this kind of cut-to-the-chase, friend-to-friend language in your interactions with Him, especially when you are in trouble.

Second, note that after he *calls* on the Lord for help in urgency, he immediately *remembers* who God is and what He has promised. This is an integral step in bolstering ourselves in the Lord. David lauds God's faithfulness, His justice, His mercy, and power. He quotes His promises to deliver, rescue, and provide, praising Him for everything He is and everything He's spoken or done in the past. Here is a perfect example of David reminding himself of all that He is to him in Psalm 18:2-3: "The LORD is my rock, my fortress, and my savior; my God is my rock, in whom I find protection. He is my shield, the strength of my salvation, and my stronghold. I will call on the LORD, who is worthy of praise, for he saves me from my enemies."

David will remind himself of His willingness and ability to perform those things again in the present situation. Notice how he recounts the promises and past actions of God on his behalf to bolster his trust:

He reached down from heaven and rescued me; he drew me out of deep waters. He delivered me from my powerful enemies, from those who hated me and were too strong for me. They attacked me at a moment when I was weakest, but the LORD upheld me. He led me to a place of safety; he rescued me because He delights in me. In your strength I can crush an army; with my

God, I can scale any wall. As for God, his way is perfect. All the Lord's promises prove true. He is a shield for all who look to him for protection, Psalm 18: 16-19, 29-33.

Third, after David saturates himself with and focuses on the majesty, faithfulness, and character of His God, he overflows with *praises*, thanking Him that He has heard his prayer and will act on his behalf. That's how we should end our prayers, with assurance in the knowledge that our Lord is responding in His love and magnificence even before we say the "Amen." Jesus instructed us, "All things for which you pray and ask, *believe* that you have received them, and they shall be granted you," Mark 11:24. Giving thanks and declaring our trust before we see the answer is evidence that we truly know our Father, and David did it well. He "let his heart take courage" and declares in confidence and with thanksgiving Who He is and what He will do:

The LORD lives! Blessed be my rock!
May the God of my salvation be exalted!
For this, O LORD, I will praise you among the nations;
I will sing joyfully to your name.
You give great victories to your king;
you show unfailing love to your anointed,
to David and all his descendants forever.
Psalm 18: 46-50

To encourage yourself in God, freely call on Him,

remember His character and offer the natural expression of praise.

David's Cliffhanger Resolved

It is a true statement that only when we get out on a limb can we reach the fruit. So it is with being on the edge of a cliff...it's there where we die or are delivered. God likes to show off His glory in these impossible situations...Daniel in the lions' den, Shadrach, Mishach, and Abednego in the fiery furnace, Esther approaching the king, Moses trapped at the Red Sea, the list goes on and on. Your story has to have a cliffhanger somewhere, too. Get ready!

David had already trained himself in the art of receiving encouragement from His Maker *before* the major crisis at Ziklag. This prepared him to respond wisely in this intense do-or-die situation. He *knew* his story would not end here. He had seen the faithfulness of God many times over. He had settled that God was absolutely trustworthy long before facing this crucible. The proclamations and the promises of God made that he was *chosen* to be the future king of Israel were unshakable. David remembered and believed them. He would not go just "halfway up the hill" of his calling. How about us? Have we hidden the word of God so firmly in our hearts that we will not be shaken?

There was a confidence built inside David that assured him that death through stoning by this angry mob of his co-workers would *not* be his portion." The LORD is my light and my salvation; Whom shall I fear? The LORD is the defense of my life; Whom shall I dread? (Psalm 27:1) was his theme song and composition. He knew what the Lord had said about him, who he was and what he was called to do. This little outburst of insanity at Ziklag was not about to upset God's promised outcome.

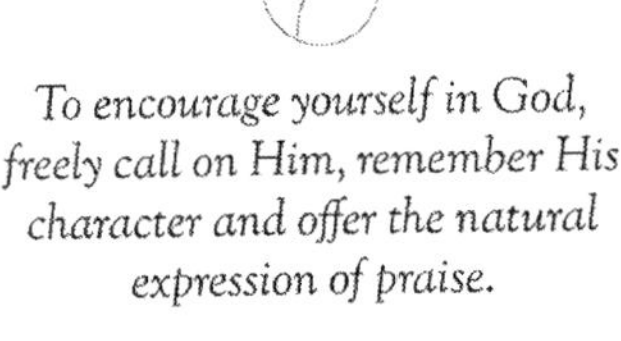

To encourage yourself in God, freely call on Him, remember His character and offer the natural expression of praise.

Pilots practice emergency procedures over and over so that when a real one erupts, they are ready and go automatically into emergency mode. Responding to challenges along the way and seeing His intervention in our lives *prepare us* for greater onslaughts and inevitable victories. As a shepherd defending the sheep from a lion and a bear, David's faith in the Mighty One grew strong. Facing and defeating Goliath in the courage of the Lord was no big deal with his eyes fixed on the Lord and His covenant word. *Everyone* in the Israeli army cowered in fear, including King Saul. But David, a person with an intimate relationship with the Lord ran toward the challenge in the power supplied by God. That same power was available to every soldier fearfully hiding from the battle.

Back to Ziglag...Although the scripture tells us that David

wept with all the men and was *very* distressed, He didn't stop there, whine or sulk or fling insults at the Lord, or ask, "Why me, Lord?" He silenced the fears and emotions and approached the Lord for specific and clear guidance as to *what* he should do in this horrendous situation before him. The future of hundreds of innocent women and children was at stake and the reputation of the God of Israel.

Another chilling aspect of this story is the irrational reaction the men with David had to this attack of the enemy. "David's mighty men" who followed him in battle *severely* failed the loyalty test. How suddenly they turned against David to blame him, instantly ready to kill him! Had they followed through, they would have *never* seen the restoration of their wives, children, and possessions. This is a strong warning for us not to turn on our spiritual leaders or one another in times of intense warfare. Standing in unity, not against one another, is God's way. Strife opens the door to every evil thing.

*For where envying and strife is, there is confusion and **every evil work**. But the wisdom that is from above is first pure, then peaceable, gentle, and easy to be intreated, full of mercy and good fruits, without partiality, and without hypocrisy. And the fruit of righteousness is sown in peace of them that make peace.*

James 3:16-18

When we face a crisis, it is vital that we remember that we can follow David's example and sincerely encourage ourselves in the Lord.

1. *Call* boldly upon Him in our distress, *knowing* He is there to respond.

2. *Remember*, remember who He is, how unfailing His love is for us and others, what He has promised, and what He has faithfully done in our life in the past. That knowledge keeps the storm on the outside, while confidence in Him keeps us at peace on the inside. We may not understand much about all the ins and outs of a present challenge, but we *do* know, "That God causes *all* things to work for good for those who love Him and are called according to His purposes," Romans 8:28. We can stand on that.

3. *Praise*, declare His praises, His goodness, and trust, and expect the operations of love in the situation. Start forming these habits now, in smaller difficulties.

We must settle it in our hearts, that as Romans 8:31 tells us, no matter what has or may come against us, God is *for* us, and as Isaiah 54:1 declares, "no weapon formed against us shall prosper." Though everything may be crumbling around us, those truths are unchanging and we can be unmoved by difficulties, fastened to Him.

We can approach the Lord with full assurance that He

will hear and answer us in times of distress. I love how David exemplifies this *full* confidence in Him, knowing that He will hear and answer him in his time of need. Although at that very moment, everyone around him was turning against him, likely starting to pick up the largest rocks they could find to throw at him, David knew what to do and where to turn. After the scripture reveals that he "encouraged himself in God," it tells us what he did next.

And David inquired of the LORD, saying, "Shall I pursue this band? Shall I overtake them?" And He said to him, "Pursue, for you shall surely overtake them, and you shall surely rescue all."(8)

David sought the Lord, who faithfully responded, giving those clear instructions and encouraging promises of success. David listened, obeyed, acted on those directives, and courageously attacked the enemy, recovering *all* that was lost.

And David slaughtered them from the twilight until the evening of the next day; and not a man of them escaped, except four hundred young men who rode on camels and fled. So David recovered all that the Amalekites had taken and rescued his two wives. But nothing of theirs was missing, whether small or great, sons or daughters, spoil or anything that they had taken for themselves; David brought it all back, I Samuel 30:17-19. (I've often wondered if later anyone apologized for the stoning idea...?)

David knew the secret of turning to God for heart strength to venture, resist opposition and prevail. He came into the crisis having already determined that God was for Him, would faithfully keep His Word to him, be His counselor, give him direction and the courage to act. Now you can follow his example. *We* can encourage ourselves in God. Not once, but throughout our walk of faith.

David would need to repeat this again and again in his life. Another fiery trial was right around the corner for him. He would hear the grievous news that Jonathan, his beloved covenant friend, had fallen in battle while fighting the Philistines with Saul. Saul had been warned that if he pursued this battle that they would die but charged ahead anyway and Jonathan, loyal to his father to the end, died with him. David's undying love is revealed so beautifully in this tribute to Saul and Jonathan. This event paradoxically was one that both caused him deep grief in losing his soul mate, but would also lead to his formal anointing to be king of Israel.

Saul and Jonathan, beloved and pleasant in their life, And in their death, they were not parted; They were swifter than eagles, They were stronger than lions. "O daughters of Israel, weep over Saul, Who clothed you luxuriously in scarlet, Who put ornaments of gold on your apparel. "How have the mighty fallen in the midst of the battle! Jonathan is slain on your high places. "I am distressed for you, my brother Jonathan; You have been very pleasant to me. Your love to me was more wonderful than the love of women." How have the mighty fallen, And the weapons of war perished!" 2 Samuel 1:23-27

We will at some time experience loss in what some have called the "dark night of the soul." And many times the outcome may be nothing like David's was at Ziklag. Maybe our experience is more like Joseph's, who was brutally rejected by his brothers, sold as a slave, falsely accused, and thrown into prison only to have a meaningful ending many years later. Perhaps we will experience the heart-wrenching passage of losing a loved one, without a clue as to why. The Lord is near to the brokenhearted and will pour out comfort in the depths of our despair. David wrote, "I *would have despaired unless I had believed* that I would see the goodness of the Lord in the land of the living. Wait for the Lord; Be strong and let your heart take courage; Yes, wait for the Lord.," Psalm 24:13-14.

Encouraging ourselves during those times is all about believing we will see the goodness of the Lord and *receiving the love of God* in the midst of the darkness, unanswered prayers, and questions. Calling out in our pain, remembering that He is still for us, and thanking Him for the eternal good that He will bring out of the worst tragedy takes courage and the deepest kind of faith. *Let* our hearts take courage. Let Him be the gentle lifter of our head, reminding us that he endured the cross for us and

His Father and ours is faithful. He will be our portion now and forever. Allow Him to demonstrate personally that He is the friend who sticks closer than any human being can...every single moment, sleepless night, or dismal day. He will abide with us and lift us up.

Facing heartbreaking times when there may not be an earthly friend or support group within our reach is inevitable. But He will always be a breath, a whisper away, ready to come to our aid and carry us through to peace even if our understanding of "why" won't come until after the grave. We can approach those hard and sometimes lonely places *knowing* that He is *for us*, has promised to work *everything* together for our good, and will faithfully instruct, guide, empower and sustain us. That's what He does best. May we take this challenge to grow in and develop the simple but vital ongoing exercise of encouraging ourselves in the Lord. Call, remember, and praise. He will carry us through every season of abandonment, loneliness, and hopelessness. He can because He's already experienced it *all* and triumphed.

BONUS BOOSTER

In the mind of God (which is the true assessment of reality) you are one with His Son and are seated positionally with Him in heavenly places far above all rule, authority, power, and dominion, and every name that is named, not only in the present age but also in the one to come. Ephesians 2:6-7

He has lifted us UP to an amazing location. We are truly looking DOWN on the powers of darkness and we rule and reign with Him.

What confidence springs from believing these verities?

Small-Group Discussion – Journal Questions

EIGHT: CHEER YOURSELF UP

Answer with a friend, a group, or individually in a journal.

1. Did you find the concept and practice of encouraging yourself at all difficult? Why?

2. Share a time when you felt completely alone with no one else to encourage you. What happened?

3. Talk about David's example. Review the 3 responses that helped him

10

HOW DID JESUS ENCOURAGE HIMSELF ON THE CROSS?

An Enlightening Study of Psalm 22

His heart was pierced many times before He was nailed to the cross.

Have you ever wondered how Jesus endured the crucifixion? The absolute, most vital destiny ever to be completed was His. Our eternal salvation hung in the balance. The culmination of God's everlasting plan hinged on these prophesied hours. His Son obediently embraced the pinnacle of all suffering to die on a criminal's cross, which was posted upon a skull-shaped hill called Golgotha. The fullness of time had arrived for redemption to be unveiled. Jesus knew His purpose. He had come to die. There was no plan B. He wrestled in prayer in the garden of Gethsemane but poignantly surrendered to His Father, "Not my will, but Yours be done," Luke 22:42. The eternal future of doomed humanity rested on those powerful seven words that reverberate eternally. *Knowing* what those seven words of surrender would require of Him, He sweat drops of blood, a rare occurrence when the human body suffers excruciating stress.

His heart was pierced *many* times before He was nailed to the cross. He was pierced by the betrayal with a kiss, all His disciples fleeing, the gruesome, merciless Roman scourging, the long, crooked thorns of mockery puncturing His skull, and the weight of the cross He was carrying. After all this agony, *then* He was hammered to the cross. What did He hear, see, feel and experience? His lacerated, bludgeoned body from the multiple, brutal lashes was now hideously held to a splintery cross by spikes piercing through his hands and feet. Slowly envision the ongoing ghastly scene all around Him painted in horrid detail here in Mark's retelling in chapter 15, verses 29-32.

- ***Those who passed by*** *derided Him, shaking their heads, "Aha, you who would destroy the temple and build it in three days, save yourself, and come down from the cross! In the same way,*
- ***The priests along with the scribes*** *were also mocking Him among themselves and saying, "He saved others; He cannot save Himself. Let the Messiah, the King of Israel come down from the cross now, so that we may see and believe."*
- ***Those who were crucified with Him*** *also taunted Him. And they cast lots to divide His clothing. And the people stood by, watching; but*
- ***The leaders*** *scoffed at Him, saying, "He saved others; let Him save Himself if He is the Messiah of God, the chosen one!"*
- ***The soldiers*** *also mocked Him, coming up and offering Him sour wine, and saying, "If you are the King of the Jews, save yourself!"*
- ***One of the criminals*** *who was hanged there kept deriding Him and saying, " Are you not the Messiah? Save yourself and us!"*

All of hell's torment was unleashed upon this innocent One making the supreme sacrifice of love. The hoards of darkness spewed out insults through willing tongues on every side. Those who passed by, the priests, the scribes, the leaders, some who were crucified with him, and the soldiers *all* united in a chorus of curses. They accused him of lying, being an imposter, making false claims to be the Messiah, and challenged Him to save Himself.

He could have saved Himself in a millisecond. He had told His disciples about that fact.

> *For this reason, the Father loves Me, because I lay down My life so that I may take it again.*
>
> *No one has taken it away from Me, but I lay it down on My own initiative.*
>
> ***I have authority to lay it down, and I have authority to take it up again.***
>
> *This commandment I received from My Father,* John 10: 17-18.

Earlier that day, when Judas came to betray Him and hand Him over to the Pharisees, Jesus asserted that *at any time* He could have easily saved Himself.

Now he who was betraying Him gave them a sign, saying, "Whomever I kiss, He is the one; seize Him."

Immediately Judas went to Jesus and said, "Hail, Rabbi!" and kissed Him. And Jesus said to him, "Friend, do what you have come for."

Then they came and laid hands on Jesus and seized Him. And behold, one of those who was with Jesus reached and drew out his sword,

*and struck the slave of the high priest and cut off his ear. Then Jesus *said to him,*

"Put your sword back into its place; for all those who take up the sword shall perish by the sword.

Or do you think that I cannot appeal to My Father, and He will at once put at My disposal more than twelve legions of angels?

How then will the Scriptures be fulfilled, which say that it must happen this way?

Jesus relied on His Father's word without wavering. He understood the higher plan of God unfolding and didn't seek to abort it. He loved us too much for that.

> *At that time Jesus said to the crowds, "Have you come out with swords and clubs to arrest Me as you would against a robber?*
>
> *Every day I used to sit in the temple teaching and you did not seize Me.*
>
> *But all this has taken place* **to fulfill the Scriptures** *of the prophets." Then all the disciples left Him and fled,* Matthew 26:48-56.

Judas betrayed Him, all His disciples left Him. He endured utter rejection and aloneness *before* He was nailed to the cross and faced the crowds of cursers. In His humanity, Jesus experienced the full spectrum of grief, desertion, and abandonment.

Pause and try to process and comprehend the depths of the pain He endured on every level...for us. We are limited in our ability to grasp this love fully, but trying to brings forth deeper adoration and waves of gratitude. Ephesians chapter 2 verse 7 states that it will take "the ages to come" for us to understand "the riches of His grace."

"Thy rebuke has broken His heart. He is full of heaviness. He looked for some to have pity on Him, but there was no man,

neither found He any to comfort Him," Psalm 69:20.

And again in Lamentations 1:12: "Behold, and see if there be any sorrow like unto His sorrow."

Never again wonder if He understands your pain and suffering. Find solace in the fact that He suffered spirit, soul, and body the entirety of every possible spectrum of oppression and pain, and can come compassionately to your aid.

It was not only the physical agony He faced enduring the most brutal Roman torture of crucifixion, or the utter abandonment by those closest to Him and the total hatred of those surrounding him with demonic defiance, but a realm of suffering even *more* intense. He was to experience the wrath of God and punishment for mankind's sins upon Himself.

For our sake, He made Him to be sin who knew no sin so that we might become the righteousness of God, 2 Corinthians 5:17.

He was wounded for our transgressions; He was crushed for our iniquities; upon Him was the chastisement that brought us peace,

and with His stripes, we are healed. All we like sheep have gone astray; we have turned every one, to his own way;

and the Lord has laid upon Him the iniquity (sin) of us all, Isaiah 53:5-6.

A broken heart full of heaviness and sorrow unsurpassed, a battered, broken body was then to absorb sin and evil and the just punishment for both on the cross. He was our substitute sacrifice, the Lamb of God taking away the sin of the world. No one but the Father understood the depths of this sacrifice. Amazing grace, amazing love. This was the great exchange: our depravity for His righteousness offered to those who believe. Breathtaking giving. Unfathomable truth. The epitome of visible love.

Very rarely will anyone die for a righteous person, though for a good person someone might possibly dare to die.

But God demonstrates his own love for us in this: While we were still sinners, Christ died for us. Romans 5:7-9 NIV

How did he encourage Himself through this foreordained sacrifice of His life? How did He literally bear the unimaginable justified wrath and condemnation for mankind's transgressions past, present, and future? Our Savior looked above and beyond to the *truest* source of encouragement through His agonizing fire. Jesus clung to the prophecies from the Old Testament containing the many references to the excruciating passion He would need to endure for us.

Psalm 22 gives us a three-dimensional, full-color glimpse into this foretold event that divides history from B.C. to A.D. This messianic, prophetic passage contains thirty-three astonishing prophecies, written hundreds of years before, that were literally fulfilled that day. Let's take an in-depth journey through this inspiring passage uncovering how Jesus found the strength to persevere, to "take courage" and complete His ordained mission. Psalm 22 reveals the majesty of the predestined plan for our rescue in full manifestation, demonstrating the absolute divine inspiration and proof of the scriptures.

Psalm 22 The Passion Translation

1 God, my God! Why would you abandon me now?

2 Why do you remain distant, refusing to answer my tearful cries in the day and my desperate cries for your help in the night?

I can't stop sobbing. Where are you, my God?

These are the well-known verses recorded in the gospels that Jesus quoted on the cross.

At three o'clock Jesus cried out with a loud voice, My God, my God, why have you forsaken me? Mark 15:34.

Large volumes of theological debate have arisen from this declaration. Did God have to abandon Him? Did He have to turn His back on Jesus because Jesus was absorbing the stench and curse of our sin, making propitiation for us? Debate continues about whether and to what degree it was necessary for the Father to temporarily withdraw from His Son for all things to be accomplished. What is certain is that scripture declares that on the cross His work was complete, justice was satisfied, and after this sacrificial and substitutionary death, "God raised Him up again, putting an end to the agony of death since it was *impossible* for Him to be held in its power," Acts 2:24. "When He raised Him from the dead and seated Him at His right hand in heavenly places," Ephesians 1:15. Jesus entered willingly into His ministry quoting the first words of Psalm 22. Like David, He practiced the first step of *calling* on the Father.

But Psalm 22 doesn't end here with the cry of anguish in the first verses.

> *3 Yet I know that you are most holy; it's indisputable.*
> *You are God-Enthroned, surrounded with songs*
> *living among the shouts of praise of your princely people.*
>
> *4 Our fathers' faith was in you, through the generations*
> *they trusted and believed in you and you came through.*

> *5 Every time they cried out to you in their despair,*
> *you were faithful to deliver them; you didn't disappoint them.*

Jesus knew the entire Psalm, not just the first few verses. He, like David, first called out to God in pain, quoting the psalm which foretold, in fine detail the sacrifice He was making and the suffering required. These next verses record the partial answer to that prayer. Verse 3 starts with, "Yet I know." What does He know about God that He can *remember* and hang on to? That God is holy, reliable, worthy of praise, and a God who in the past was faithful to deliver in times of distress.

I believe Jesus was meditating *on the entire passage* to find the strength to endure. He was *remembering* His faithful Father's indisputable character. *He called; then He remembered.* This next portion of scripture predicted his suffering as the Lamb of God for our sins in intricate detail. This supernatural portion of scripture predicting what was happening *right then* to Jesus contained the *real power* to encourage him in his intense suffering, reminding Him of the Father's predestined purpose in it.

6 But look at me now; I am like a woeful worm, crushed, and I'm bleeding crimson. I don't even look like a man anymore.
I've been abused, despised, and scorned by everyone!

The Hebrew word used here for "worm," "tola," explodes with revelation. The tola worm was known in the east for its distinct crimson blood when crushed. It was a very precious worm collected and crushed to specifically dye the garments of *royalty*. Jesus was being "crushed" for us and His royal crimson blood would "dye" the garments of His future family in the gift of His imputed righteousness. Isaiah 61:10 foretold this glorious salvation to come: "I rejoice greatly in the Lord, I exult in my God; for He has clothed me with the garments of salvation and wrapped me in a robe of righteousness." [1]

The statement, "I am a tola worm" was declaring what benefit would result from His shed blood to His church. This was the joy that allowed Him to persevere. *For the joy set before Him, he endured the cross despising the shame.* Hebrews 12:2

1. http://letusreason.org/Biblexp380.htm

7 Mocked by their jeers, despised with their sneers, as all the people poke fun at me, spitting their insults,

8 saying, "Is this the one who trusted in God? Is this the one who claims God is pleased with him?

Now let's see if your God will come to your rescue! We'll just see how much he delights in you!"

The deformation of his body that resulted from the estimated thirty-nine lashes inflicted by the Romans was prophesied and fulfilled. The mockery of the people in very specific quotes were also foretold and fulfilled. And so much more. Recalling this portion of Psalm 22 imparted hope and courage to Christ that He was fulfilling *everything* planned from before the foundation of the world. Scriptures and the Holy Spirit within had prepared him for every aspect of the dramatic divine scenario.

9 Lord, you delivered me safely from my mother's womb.

You are the one who cared for me ever since I was a baby.

10 Since the day I was born, I've been placed in your custody.
You've cradled me throughout my days.
I've trusted in you and you've always been my God.

11 So don't leave me now; stay close to me!
For trouble is all around me and there's no one else to help me.

12 I'm surrounded by many violent foes;
mighty forces of evil are swirling around me
who want to break me to bits and destroy me.

13 Curses pour from their mouths!
They're like ravenous, roaring lions tearing their prey.

These references to the onslaught of evil spirits sent to torment Him were manifesting right before His eyes and ears. Jesus, in meditating upon and quoting from this prophetic psalm was drawing strength in the Father's sovereignty and identifying Himself as the promised Redeemer spoken of centuries before. Oh the power of the living Word of God!

This supernatural portion of scripture predicting what was happening right then to Jesus contained the real power to encourage him in his intense suffering, reminding Him of the Father's predestined purpose in it.

14 Now I'm completely exhausted; I'm spent.
Every joint of my body has been pulled apart.
My courage has vanished and
my inward parts have melted away.
*15 **I'm so thirsty and parched**—dry as a bone.*
My tongue sticks to the roof of my mouth.
And now you've left me in the dust for dead.
*16 They have **pierced my hands and my feet**. Like a pack*
of wild dogs, they tear at me, swirling around me with
their hatred. They gather around me like lions to pin my
hands and feet.

The insatiable thirst, the literal piercing of hands and feet with giant nails, and the dislocation of joints are all a part of this Roman execution torture. Jesus was fully experiencing what was foretold over two hundred years before. He could recall the details of His suffering being fulfilled in exact detail.

> *17 All my bones stick out.*
> *Look at how they all gloat over me and stare!*
>
> *18 With a toss of the dice, **they divide my clothes among themselves,***
> *gambling for my garments!*

"They cast their lots to divide His clothing," Luke 23:24. This too was being executed. Another proof to Him and the world of God's predestined and recorded description of the event being carried out in every facet and detail.

> *19 Lord, my God, please don't stay far away.*
> ***For you are my only might and strength.***
> *Won't you come quickly to my rescue?*
>
> *20 Give me back my life.*
> *Save me from this violent death.*

Save my precious one and only
from the power of these demons!

21 Save me from all the power of the enemy,
from this roaring lion raging against me
and the power of his dark horde.

"Give me back my life...Save me from all the power of the enemy" carried the eternal promise of His soon deliverance. God would faithfully be liberating Him from all the evil surrounding His Son. The Father had established the perfect timing for the greatest victory of all eternity: deliverance from and the conquering of death. "Oh death, where is your sting? Oh grave, where is thy victory?" 1 Corinthians 15:55. This sacrificial death of our Savior on the cross opened the door for the mighty resurrection to follow...His and ours!

Jesus called, Jesus remembered and Jesus praised.

22 I will praise your name before all my brothers;
as my people gather I will praise you in their midst.

23 Lovers of Yahweh, praise him!
Let all the true seed of Jacob glorify him with your praises.
Stand in awe of him, all you princely people,
the offspring of Israel!

24 For he has not despised my cries of deep despair.
He's my first responder to my sufferings,
and he didn't look the other way when I was in pain.

Jesus praised His Father. His Father knew the sufferings of His crucifixion, His Father listened to the song of the afflicted. His Father didn't despise Him or ignore His pain. On the contrary, He heard *every* cry and felt *every* pang of pain!

25 You're the reason for my praise; it comes from you and goes to you.

I will keep my promise to praise you before all who fear you among the congregation of your people.

26 I will invite the poor and broken,
and they will come and eat until satisfied.
Bring Yahweh praise and you will find him.
Your hearts will overflow with life forever!

Hearts that would live forever? This is a clear reference to eternal life that would be made available even to the Gentiles through the work of the blood-stained cross. Scripture records in Hebrews 12:2 that "For the joy set before Him, He endured the cross, scorning its shame, and sat down at the right hand of the throne of God." What was the joy set before him? It was His future family! It was everyone who would come to Him and receive everlasting life through His persevering victory on the cross. Knowing that our future rebirth was being purchased forever is what helped sustain Him.

27 From the four corners of the earth,
the peoples of the world will remember and return to

Yahweh.
Every nation will come and worship him.
28 For Yahweh is King of all, who takes charge of all the nations.
29 The wealthy of this world will feast in fellowship with him
right alongside the humble of heart,
bowing down to the dust, forsaking their own souls.
They will all come and worship this worthy King!
30 His spiritual seed shall serve him.
Future generations will hear from us
about the wonders of the Victorious Lord.
31 His generation yet to be born will glorify him.
And they will all declare, "It is finished!"

> *"It is finished" was not a cry of defeat, but a shout of victory that the work of redemption was complete!*

It is finished. The Bible records that Jesus also quoted the *final* verse from Psalm 22:31 on the cross. Many do not make the connection that He quoted the beginning and the end of this messianic prophetic psalm. Knowing the exact portion of scripture He quoted makes all the difference. "It is finished" was not a cry of defeat, but a shout of victory that the work of redemption was complete!

I believe the Son of Man was infused with power from every one of these divine declarations from the start to finish of Psalm 22.

Jesus was encouraging Himself through the power of His Father's forever, settled Word about His present crucible and future victory.

He was enabled to cry out in victory announcing to heaven and hell in His last earthly breath that, "*It is finished!*"

He had performed His Father's will *every* step of the way. He had accomplished *everything* necessary for us to be reconciled to His Father.

This was the crowning victory of all ages. All glory to Him forever and ever.

I include the lyrics from "How Deep the Father's Love For Us" by Selah, which captures beautifully my gratitude and His unfathomable and magnificent love demonstrated on the cross.

How Deep The Father's Love For Us

-Selah

How deep the Father's love for us
How vast beyond all measure

That He should give His only Son
To make a wretch His treasure
How great the pain of searing loss
The Father turns His face away
As wounds that mar the Chosen One
Bring many sons to glory
Behold the man upon a cross
My sin upon His shoulders
Ashamed, I hear my mocking voice
Call out among the scoffers
It was my sin that held Him there
Until it was accomplished
His dying breath has brought me life
I know that it is finished
I will not boast in anything
No gifts, no power, no wisdom
But I will boast in Jesus Christ
His death and resurrection
Why should I gain from His reward?
I cannot give an answer
But this I know with all my heart
His wounds have paid my ransom

In light of this most wondrous triumph, we are exhorted to *fix our eyes on Him*, the author and finisher of our faith and in total dependence, run *our* race with endurance. Take time and re-read Psalm 22 with a fresh understanding of the providential plan of God revealing with astonishing detail what His Son would experience in spirit, soul, and body for our salvation. Reinforce how our Savior drew the ultimate strength to complete His mission. May this give us renewed courage to finish the course He has set out before us. Through every heartbreak, rejection, or abandonment we may face, we are *never* alone, we can take courage and *everything* we need directly from calling upon, remembering, and praising the Sovereign Lord and His reliable words, just as David and Christ our Lord, Himself did.

BONUS BOOSTER

Christ in you is the hope of glory, and when He looks at you He sees Jesus. And when He looks at Jesus, He sees you!

"The mystery of the ages is Christ in you, the hope of glory," Colossians 1:27

Every area of our life changes when we fully embrace the fact of our supernatural union with Him.

Christ living in and through you is God's hope of being seen and glorified. SELAH

Small-Group Discussion – Journal Questions

NINE: HOW DID JESUS ENCOURAGE HIMSELF ON THE CROSS?

Answer with a friend, a group, or individually in a journal.

1. What insights follow knowing He was quoting from this psalm during the most agonizing experience ever gone through by anyone?

2. Reread Psalm 22 together and highlight specific prophecies being fulfilled, using this guide.

The following is a list of 17 prophecies being fulfilled in Psalm 22 of Jesus' Crucifixion:

- He will be forsaken by God: Psalm 22:1
- Die during the afternoon: Psalm 22:2
- He will be despised: Psalm 22:6
- Observers disgusted with Him: Psalm 22:7
- Observers will mock Him: Psalm 22:8
- He will be Born to die: Psalm 22:9-10
- Die from a ruptured heart: Psalm 22:13-17
- He will thirst: Psalm 22:13-17
- Psalm 22:16
- His hands and feet, pierced: Psalm 22:16

- Naked before the world: Psalm 22:17-18
- Clothing gambled for: Psalm 22:18
- He will commit Himself to God: Psalm 22:19-21
- Destroy the works of the devil: Psalm 22:20-21
- The meaning of love, defined: Psalm 22:22
- His death wins Him Rulership: Psalm 22:27-29
- Eyewitnesses will record this: Psalm 22:30-31

[2]

2. How were these details important for Jesus to encourage Himself on the cross?

3. How does studying the entirety of this psalm shed a different light upon Christ's words on the cross?

4. Discuss how Jesus' example of trusting entirely upon God's word can impact your life.

5. Have a time of worship, perhaps celebrate communion together and extol the great work of Christ on the cross for you.

2. https://robertcliftonrobinson.com/publications/the_prophecies_of_the_messiah/365-prophecies-by-book/psalms-2/psalms/psalms-prophecies-11-20/prophecy-78/

11

HOW TO PRACTICE UP AND TRAIN YOUR TONGUE

The Sovereign One Wants Your Ear and Your Tongue

The Sovereign Lord has given Me the tongue of disciples,
that I may know how to sustain the weary one with a word.
He awakens Me morning by morning,
He awakens My ear to listen as a disciple.
The Lord GOD has opened My ear;
And I was not disobedient, Nor did I turn back,
Isaiah 50:4.

Now for some very down-to-earth instruction. Why did our Lord suffer so intensely for our reconciliation? Part of His joy was knowing He would no longer live in temples made of human hands but in His people, His church. Because we have been forgiven, justified, and made new, we are qualified by His blood to be vessels for Him to literally indwell. His purpose in this new dwelling place is *to be seen in us*, live through us, and reach out through us to those still waiting to hear and embrace the good news of the cross. Our active taking on and fulfilling our God-assignments makes the results of His sacrifice expand.

Behold the practical outworking of this "mystery of the ages, which is Christ in you," Colossians 1:27. This majestic verse from Isaiah above gives specific insight and instructions about how we can be a transmitter of God's encouragement. In context, this is a messianic passage about the ministry of Jesus. But it directly applies to believers, too, in whom He lives and through whom He speaks. We can clearly see how He operated his life and ministry and enter into the same people-blessing ministry. Let's dig deeper into this incredible verse that unveils such a beautiful lifestyle offered to us.

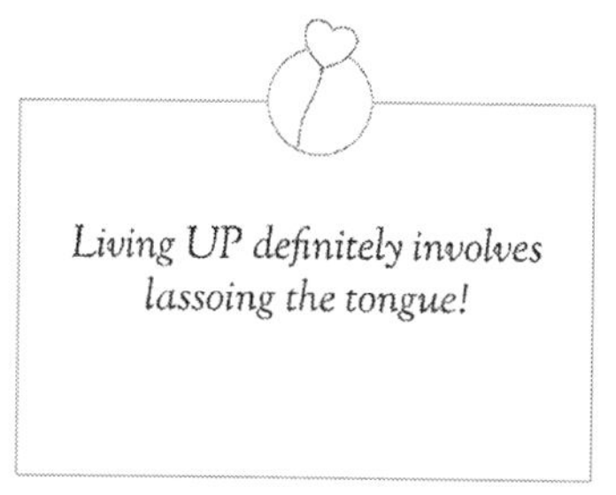

Living UP definitely involves lassoing the tongue!

"The Sovereign Lord has given Me the tongue of disciples, that I may know how to sustain the weary one with a word." The King James version uses the expression "tongue of the learned." God is after our tongues in a big way. "Death and life are in the power of the tongue and those who love it will eat its fruit," Proverbs 18:21. The person whose tongue yields to God is called a perfect or mature person. "For we all stumble in many things. If anyone does not stumble in word, he is a perfect man, able also to bridle the whole body," James 3:2. Our Maker knows the power of encouraging or destructive words. He desires to use our tongue for life-building purposes. When we allow Him to harness our words to agree with His; we can speak with a "learned" tongue. When we discipline our words and pick up the language of lifting others, our tongue becomes His. Why does He "give the tongue of disciples"? To know how to "sustain the weary one with a word." He wants to give us words to speak with *one focus* in mind: the uplifting and sustaining of those around us who are weary. This melts my heart when I read the love between the lines here. He has a strong desire for encouragement to come to every person who is weary and down. That includes you and me.

Who can ever plumb the depths of the love of God? Our tongues need PRACTICE to become "learned".

No one is useless in this world who lightens the burdens of others.

-Charles Dickens

Our study of the inflow of encouragement now turns to understanding the vital *outflow* of this powerful dynamism. Do you know why the Dead Sea is dead? Because waters only run *into* it, but never out. If we are only takers, we also become dead, stagnant seas. Becoming a vessel that splashes others with the refreshment He pours into us is the highest fulfillment of Christ living in and through us.

I enjoy noticing what people display on their refrigerators or around their workplaces. *Never* have I seen a framed copy of someones "You're fired" memo, a failed test, a"Dear John" letter, or any other painful reminder of life's many downers. We strive to forget those. Instead, there are "I Love You!" notes, snapshots of catching the big Marlin, "Thinking of you!" post-its, children's crayon masterpieces, and photos of best friends and family. This patchwork, encouragement gallery we display *shouts* something about our nature. We *recharge* with these tangible expressions and images of joy and affirmation.

Positive comments and actions can *truly* change someone's day or at least bring a momentary smile to it. To a stranger or intimate friend, since my Father God has poured out His love into my life, I've decided to risk being openly encouraging to extend those uplifting galleries beyond the refrigerator. *No* one will perish from sincere edification. And not one person has ever yelled at me for passing on kind words and compliments. Oh, I have my days being self-absorbed, busy with my to-do list. Those are the wasted, un-sparkling days I wish I could live over. I would much rather experience a Lemon-Lime Perrier day focusing on lifting others with a learned tongue of a disciple.

Encouragement is like a contagious virus. Prayers, words, and kind actions spread it. Once someone is infected, the virus spreads quickly and exponentially. Observe this chain reaction. A husband says (quite unexpectedly), "You are such a babe," to his wife, who was feeling gloomy about her recent gain of a few pounds, but now finds herself smiling. She walks a little lighter in mood into their teenaged daughter's wall-to-wall, cluttered bedroom, and instead of venting her disgust, slips out with, "How's my dear and brilliant girl this day?" The daughter turns over in bed with a surprised look on her face, and while thinking to herself, "Who are *you*: and *what* have you done with my mother?" manages a conceding, "Fine, mom, and I promise to find my carpet underneath the clothes today."

Maybe it doesn't *always* work this magically or instantly, but uplifting words do exactly what the word means: *lift!* They fill the atmosphere with hope and creative power. We've all seen the opposite work. Grumpiness and negativity can invade a place like a skunk's odor, and suddenly everyone in the room is knee-deep in quicksand, sinking further and further into a pool of pessimism. How often have we gone through a day in the black goop of depression? Too often.

In my early years of teaching high school, I would despise going into the teacher's lounge if a particular group of teachers was there.

"That Jimmy is so stupid, and I am insulted that he wants extra help from me...I don't have time for slow learners," one chain-smoking teacher would vomit.

"I just don't know when the administration is going to wake up to the inane policies we have to follow," another disgruntled man would begin.

It was like there was an ongoing competition for who could be the most disgusted and critical of everything and everyone. This derogative disease is contagious and slimes everyone in its presence. The peer pressure to be cynical was heavy. Most teachers crumbled under it and joined in the dirge. I was stifled and sickened by it. The story of the massive amount of Israelites bit and killed by venomous snakes sent in the wilderness (Numbers 21:6) because of their griping and complaining jerks my chain when I am tempted to grumble.

A brand new teacher, I sincerely enjoyed being in the classroom with my students. Although probably naïve to the many challenges ahead, I surely wouldn't look to any of these professional whiners for inspiration. I resisted a strong urge to scream out, "Doesn't anybody have anything *good* to say about the students, the faculty, or the administration of this school? No wonder the students don't like your classes!" But that would be stooping, becoming negative about their negativity so I usually just slipped out and ate my lunch with a few of my endearing sophomore students. We had much more interesting conversations.

Challenge: It's like learning a foreign language

These teachers became fluent in the language of fussing and fault-finding through repeated years of practice. Complaining is well-practiced all around us, almost a national pastime. To turn the tide, we desperately need to develop a new habit through *intentional* practice. Do an experiment and see how often during an hour or a day you find yourself inviting snake bites by complaining inwardly or outwardly. It might be shocking. Living UP definitely involves lassoing the tongue!

The definition of practice helps. It is "the application and implementation of a belief, idea or theory: the *repeated* performance of a skill in order to acquire and maintain proficiency." The world is *full* of proficient gurus of the gloomy and masters of the morose. Encouragement proficients are the exception.

We can learn to speak a new language of inspiration. But like learning a foreign language, we will have to apply ourselves, master the vocabulary of encouragement, and rehearse daily until we become fluent.

A little more introspection is required here. Would your close friends and family say you are usually an encouraging person to be around? It might surprise you to know the truth. Everyone goes through tough times and needs to process verbally at times. That's okay. But relatively speaking, are you usually able to focus your attention outside of yourself? Those who narcissistically talk only about themselves make others want to leave the one-track conversation. From the eyes of others who know you, how often do they see you walking around with a black cloud over your head? We joke in our family about being at times too much like "Eeyore," that down-in-the-dumps donkey from the classic Winnie the Pooh stories. Eeyore oozes negativity and depressing phrases like, "It looks like earthquake weather again," and "Thanks for noticing me."

Analyze yourself. Are you more often critical or uplifting? Acquiring a new language will allow us to change our inner dialogue and outward conversation. Although it can be a challenge to change directions and swim cheerfully upstream, it's *not* impossible. No need to become the bluebird of happiness, but make an intelligent decision to follow the wisdom in Ephesians 4:29. "Let *no* unwholesome word proceed out of your mouth, but *only* that which brings edification, according to the need of the moment in order so that it will bring grace to those who hear." That is a high bar command from scripture. Applying it literally would remove a majority of our words.

We *can* learn to speak a new language of inspiration. But like learning a foreign language, we will have to apply ourselves, master the vocabulary of encouragement, and rehearse daily until we become fluent. Factors that determine how fast learning will take place center on two key facts: how much *time* a student will commit *each day* to learn and how often a student will *practice*. The common thread of research confirms that the best results include studying and practicing a few minutes each day. Pretty simple. Daily, a few minutes. No cramming, just daily practice, daily review, and positive progress follows. We really *can* master a new language, the language of heaven.

According to the US Department of State Foreign Service Institute, the classroom hours required to gain a high intermediate level varies from easy languages (575-600 hours) to hard languages (2200 hours). Mastering the language of edification probably falls into the "hard" category, but God's Spirit, the Encourager inside us, will supply all the power we need to fulfill the Ephesians 4:29 standard. Let's take the challenge.

1

Words are like seeds, and when they are kindly planted and watered will bring a crop of blessing. "But *encourage* one another *daily*, as long as it is called "Today," so that none of you may be hardened by sin's deceitfulness," Hebrews 3:13. Our harnessed tongue becomes His tool to sustain the weary and potentially sin-hardened all around us.

Encouraging believers was the number one goal of Paul's many visits. "For I long to see you so that I may impart some spiritual gift to you, that you may be established;

1. (http://www.openculture.com/2017/11/a-map-showing-how-much-time-it-takes-to-learn-foreign-languages-from-easiest-to-hardest.html)

that is, that I may be encouraged together with you while among you, each of us by the other's faith, both yours and mine," Romans 1:11-12. He echoes this *priority* in his letter to the church at Thessalonica: "Therefore encourage one another, and build up one another, just as you also are doing," 1 Thessalonians 5:11. How revolutionizing it would be if more we and others in our family, church, work, and the community took this exhortation seriously? Becoming bilingual with life-giving communication from heaven will transform our environment and the lives we touch. Even a handful fluent in this language of love with "the tongue of disciples" could impact the entire world.

Don't forget the kids: they learn foreign languages the easiest!

For the rest of his life, Oliver Twist remembers
a single word of blessing spoken to him by another child
because this word stood out so strikingly
from the consistent discouragement around him.
-Charles Dickens, Oliver Twist

It is a fact that children exposed to another language in the early years learn it with high speed and fluency. I believe the language of encouragement should be modeled and fostered in the home. Children will naturally imitate the family of origin lingo.

Kids are open to expressing words of love if that practice has been exemplified. I love the Dickens' quote about Oliver Twist that *one word* of blessing that came from another child imprinted upon his life, and it stood firm amid his day-to-day, discouragement-centered culture. Parents and teachers can capitalize upon this at home and in the classroom and create activities that call for kids to practice blessing others. Teens make great candidates, too.

Our church youth group once adopted a favorite tradition worth passing on. Every day between Thanksgiving and Christmas, each of them would try to cease all complaining and do at least *one* act of random kindness for family, friends, or strangers. Each week they would gather and share their euphoric excitement about what they had done and the joyous outcome of their actions. They were very creative and did everything from chores for their siblings, extra acts of service around the home, opening doors for shoppers at the mall, greeting people, handing out free water bottles with cool quotes attached to them, walking a neighbor's dog to making brownies for lonely teens at school who were sitting alone in the lunchroom. This annual youth group activity succeeded in several ways. Having teens experience the joy of focusing off of themselves and on to others had a significant impact on *them* as much as on those whom they randomly blessed. It soon became one of their favorite holiday traditions.

Let's teach our children and teens the beautiful language of kindness and encouragement. It will set them on a path of favor and blessing. Our family found a powerful and practical tool to help build a culture of support in our home and relationship circles. Every birthday we started the practice of sharing "Silver Boxes," verbal gifts of blessing with one another. Special credit is given to Florence Littauer who authored the book *Silver Boxes, the gift of Encouragement* from which this term and empowering concept was learned. Here is another story about our "almost missed miracle" daughter growing up.

Chop Sticks and Silver Boxes Flash Back

Let no one ever come to you without leaving better and happier.
-Mother Teresa

Red dragons, delicate Asian fans, ivory chopsticks, and red and yellow Chinese lanterns decorated the table for Hannah's 8th birthday. It was her idea to have a Chinese theme, peeked by her interest in the country of her birth. Her carefully copied black Chinese calligraphy symbols proudly hung taped all over the walls. Ten, giggling girlfriends in red and turquoise silk surrounded the glowing, birthday girl. French-braided by her adoring older sister, her long black hair in an intricate bun was attached with carved, bone-colored, chopsticks.

"We have a Porter birthday tradition we invite you all to share in," I instructed the honored guests. "Before we have cake, we like to give the birthday person a special kind of gift. It's a gift that stays in the heart all year long. This gift is called a "silver box." It is a very valuable present, more precious than silver. You each take turns to tell Hannah something that you admire or like about her or recall a special memory that you cherish with her. These are gifts made of words and wrapped with love. They never rust or break as they are forever stored in the heart."
Hannah matter-of-factly added, "Who wants to go first?"

"Well, I like Hannah because she helps me when I'm sad," remarked a younger friend thoughtfully.

"I like Hannah... because she's funny," chuckled another.

"Hannah is my BEST friend," exclaimed still another.

"I'm glad to have Hannah in my life...'cause..." a long pause punctuated this poignant moment, "she's one of my Chinese sisters," giggled another shyly. This beautiful girl along with several others at our festive table was adopted on the same unforgettable day as Hannah when ten families traveled together to China to claim our precious little ones. Our group of families maintained a relationship through the earlier years so that our girls could have some sense of extended family and friendship with girls from their place of birth. Those unique words echoed around the table by the other Asian beauties. The moment was magical. To think that these Chinese "sisters" lived through the horror of abandonment, squalid conditions in their orphanages (some had severe levels of lead in their blood when first adopted) to blossom into the radiant and bright 8-year-olds who now exchanged sincere, loving words on this occasion was overwhelming.

Like living scrapbooks of their blurry, painful past, each had defied death and created new pages of colorful, childhood joy and love. Love and belonging were bridging their desolate beginnings to further pages of nurture and unlimited potential. Tears spontaneously escaped from this mother's eyes. One by one, each bosom-buddy was able to share a little sincere compliment with Hannah which strengthened the bond of their friendship. Family members chimed in with endearing blessings and affirmations.

"I'm SO glad God let me be your daddy," confirmed Bruce with watery eyes.

"Me too," Hannah giggled, satisfied and beaming at what was now an expected highlight of every birthday.

"Hannah, God gave me the best little sister in the world when He gave me you, Boo," Naomi said with a big smile. Hannah nodded her head in pleased agreement. "Now for the cake!" she commanded.

This Silver Box tradition is the pinnacle point of every birthday, Mother's or Father's Day or holiday gathering. Exchanging valid words of affection and fondness have us crying and laughing as we connect hearts again. No one has ever died of too much love. No matter our age, there is a place inside each one of us just waiting to be hugged verbally. Sometimes uncomfortable silences precede these silver boxes, as we steer our brains in a positive direction preparing to share, but we all need to practice and perfect this almost lost art.

Many years now after her eighth birthday party, the other presents have been lost, broken, or gone out of style. But the loving silver boxes live on forever in her heart, answering "Yes" to the most important questions she will ever ask when confronting her challenging beginnings, "Am I loved?" and "Do I matter?"

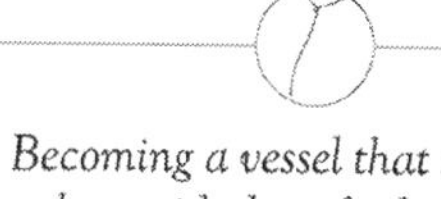

Becoming a vessel that splashes others with the refreshment He pours into us is the highest fulfillment of Christ living in and through us.

We include this silver box exercise of appreciating others intentionally with words of affirmation in our casual house church gatherings. We have determined never to hesitate to tell members how we love and value them. Life gets heavy and hard at times. We need to hear from one another those expressions that hearten and inspire *before* a funeral. Try a round of silver boxes at your next family or friend gathering. Watch how the "magic" visibly lifts the people for whom you care.

BONUS BOOSTER

There is not only the head of Christ seated next to the Father, but the head and the body! That means you!

"And God put everything under His feet and made Him head over everything for the church, which is His body, the fullness of Him who fills all in all," *Ephesians 1:23*

Small-Group Discussion – Journal Questions

TEN: PRACTICE UP

1. Reflect on what it means to be the indwelling place of Christ on the earth.

2. Have you ever tried to learn a foreign language? What difficulties did you face?

3. How would you evaluate the negative or encouraging culture in your family growing up?

4. Read Hebrews 3:13. Why does scripture admonish us to encourage each other DAILY?

5. Read Ephesians 4:29 and put it in your own words. Renew your commitment to follow this with your words this week and beyond.

6. Have a time practicing giving your group or family "Silver Boxes." Share the experience.

12

HOW TO LISTEN UP AND LIFT OTHERS

The Sovereign One Wants Your Ear and Your Tongue

The Sovereign Lord has given Me the tongue of disciples,
that I may know how to sustain the weary one with a word.
He awakens Me morning by morning,
He awakens My ear to listen as a disciple.
The Lord GOD has opened My ear;
And I was not disobedient, Nor did I turn back,
Isaiah 50:4.

Let's return to this dynamic scripture. "That I may know how to sustain the weary."

Synonyms for "weary" are: tired out, exhausted, worn out, drained, and disillusioned. Who do you know like that? The Lord wants to transmit life-giving words through you that will sustain them. Synonyms for "sustain" are: carry on, keep going, uphold, support, and encourage. He passes words from His heart through us. Those words will bring comfort and strength to those in our circle of influence who are drained and about to give up. All it costs is a little time to hear and then obediently share those God-breathed words. These kindnesses could cause them to get up and run an important race for God which in turn benefits all the people in their circle of influence. This chain reaction is so powerful. The eternal impact of that one encouraged life will have a ripple effect on lives we'll never meet. How inspiring it is knowing that He spoke through us to supply the tank of gas necessary to help others speed ahead.

After our tongue takes lessons, what else? "He awakens Me morning by morning; He awakens My ear to listen as a disciple." You give attention to your ears *as well as* your tongue. Jesus talked often about the necessity of having ears to hear. He wasn't talking about physical hearing, but spiritual hearing. Hearing God's still small voice is another skill you can develop. Saturating your mind with His written Word is the best and safest way to acquaint yourself with what He thinks, says, and does. Everything He may impress on your spiritual ears when you listen will line up with it 100%.

"Being" with Him through daily fellowship creates more sensitivity to Him. He always draws from and shares the great and precious promises recorded in scripture. The Holy Spirit brings to our remembrance everything that is relevant to our lives and others. We recognize His voice just like a familiar friend who calls us on the phone. Jesus said, "My sheep hear My voice, and I know them, and they follow Me," John 10:27. We begin to hear from Him more than we realize.

He wants to give us words to speak with one focus in mind: the uplifting and sustaining of those around us who are weary.

Just awaken each morning, stop and *listen* as a disciple. I have noticed that if I listen intently to the Lord when I am just coming out of sleep, I am more sensitive to His promptings. I direct my first thoughts toward Him in thanksgiving. I mentally take a shower in His love and presence, allowing myself to be filled afresh with His Spirit. I must suppress my inclination to focus on my "to-do list" for the day and first interact with my closest Friend. I ask Him for any names of "weary ones" on His heart that I should reach out to that day. It helps if

I jot down a note, or otherwise, His instructions may fade from my memory and I might miss a divine opportunity.

With hearkening and practice, I can hear those names He will drop into my mind or heart. The message He wants me to pass on bubbles up, and I just "know" what to share. These messages of life may come right as I am lying there, as I read the scripture or at any time throughout the day. Sometimes these impressions come as I sit down to text, email, call or write them. The important thing is for me to *listen*, and make myself available to be a lifter of others. Often it doesn't take minutes, but just seconds to listen. If nothing or no one comes to mind, I go on my way keeping my ears open to His voice as people cross my path that day.

"I did not turn back..."

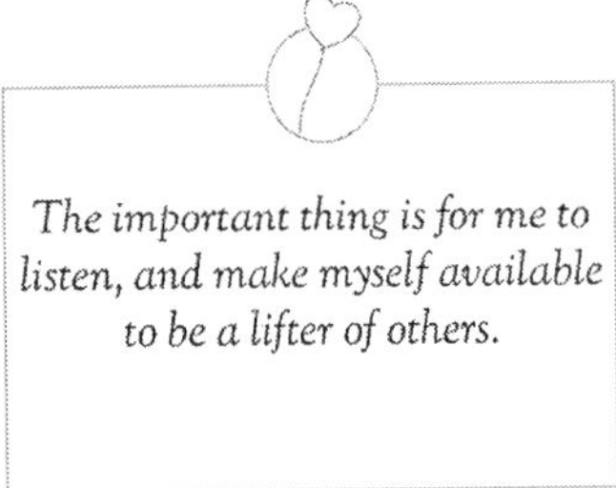

Then, I must be obedient to *give* the word that He gave me. "The Lord God has opened My ear, And I was not disobedient, Nor did I turn back." The King James version is more explicit here: "The Lord God has given me the tongue of the learned, that I should *know how* to speak a word in season to him who is weary." Get the direction and love message, follow through and deliver. God's communications are "in season" meaning significant in a specific time frame. Time is often of the essence in the delivery of these jewels. I am grateful when somebody calls me precisely when I am sinking into despair. Perhaps our message for someone is not an emergency, but it will be the perfect divine RX for them at that moment or prepare them for something coming. I've been on the receiving end, and I'll never forget the impact.

How do you start the conversation? Keep it casual and heartfelt. You don't have to say, "Thus saith the Lord," intimidating the recipient. I like to preface my remarks with something like, "You have been on my mind, and I felt impressed to get in touch with you." Or I may ask, "How have you been doing lately? I can't stop thinking about you."

One of my friends practices this by giving flowers to the one she was impressed with to remind her of God's love. What woman wouldn't love that? It may be that individuals open up and allow you to pray for them. Prayer is a great gift as well. Just calling someone to remind them that we love them, that we were thinking about them, and that God is faithful to them can do the job. Sometimes the Lord may want us to drop in and say, "Hi," and demonstrate His love. Keep it simple and follow your heart. He lives there and will do the rest. We will be amazed at some of the responses we will get like, "How did you know I was so down?" or "You won't believe this, but I just prayed and asked God about the very thing you are sharing with me," or "How did you know I just got a concerning report from my doctor?" I don't think there is any greater joy than knowing we have been a messenger of the Lord to touch someone's life profoundly and directly.

People who have passed into heaven live in continuous exaltation and full-color knowledge of His beauty and goodness. On earth our vision is blurred; we see through a dark mirror and a maze of confusion. But as we gaze at Him in His Word and accept the honor of transmitting those messages, we bring light to the darkness. Our words and actions already communicate some kind of message daily. Why not let the message be *good* news.

Here are a few examples of this Isaiah 50:4 ministry principle in action.

Who Wrote Handel's Messiah?

"A word of encouragement during a failure is worth more than an hour of praise after success."
-Author Unknown

This sounds like a trick question. The fame of George Handel and his oratorio, "The Messiah" is well known. But have you ever heard of a man named Charles

Jennens? Without this unsung hero in Handel's life, there would be no such glorious masterpiece.

Charles Jennens was a wealthy landowner and devout Protestant believer who lived from 1700 to 1773. He was a great patron of the Arts and lover of Handel's music. When Handel was recovering from a stroke, out of favor with the latest musical tastes of London, bankrupt, profoundly depressed, and facing debtor's prison, Jennens, a true friend, stepped up to change the direction of his career and life. He knew what a terrible loss it would be if Handel and his God-given musical genius languished the rest of his years in prison. Jennens true friendship in the time of need was a lifeline to rescue him literally. The power of his encouragement and engagement in Handel's life during this period of despair is an unforgotten page of history.

Jennens believed in Handel when no one else did. He had an inspired plan. The two had collaborated on other works, but little did they know that this next one would become the most far-reaching, famous of all. Concerned about British society's departure from biblical Christian beliefs by embracing Deism and Rationalism, Charles had created a libretto or "text" for an oratorio completely using scriptures from the Old and New Testament that conveyed the entire plan of salvation, the deity of Christ, and the proof that Jesus was the prophesied Messiah. He believed that God's eternal Word coupled with the gifts of composing that he knew Handel possessed would be the most powerful way to influence his world. Little did he conceive that he would be impacting not only present society but many generations to come.

He approached George Handel with this opportunity and urged him to give himself to composing all the music for this epic oratorio. He gave it to him totally for free, wanting to remain entirely anonymous on his part. After a short time of convincing, Handel agreed, even in his weakened state of health and hope, to devote himself to this significant creation. Handel became so absorbed, energized, and inspired that he rarely ate, drank, or slept. In the dim candlelight which damaged his sight in later years, he passionately engaged his God-breathed gifts to the metamorphosis of scripture into music. He completed the composition of this entire masterpiece of 262 hand-scripted pages in 23 days! This was a profoundly spiritual experience for Handel. One evening his loyal and unpaid servant went to force him to take just a glass of milk for sustenance and found him weeping in the dark on the ground. Fearing he was dying, he approached him. Handel, through tears, had just written the "Hallelujah Chorus" and told his servant, "I did think I did saw all Heaven before me, and the great God himself." His kind servant knew that something quite unprecedented and extraordinary had taken place.

Living then in Dublin, Ireland, Handel performed "Messiah" near Easter in 1742 at St. Patrick's Cathedral and several other halls. The performances raised funds for orphans, and the needy, and freed several men from debtor's prison. Four hundred pounds were raised one night helping the foundling homes he worked with and paying for the release of 142 men from debtor's prison.

The fame of this masterpiece became so popular in Ireland that women were encouraged to leave their hoop slips behind and men their swords to fit more in the audience for these charity events. The impact of this electrifying combination of the Word of God with Handel's God-given talent spread like heavenly wildfire.

A year later, Handel was invited to return to London to present his famous oratorio to the King. So moved was King George II that during the performance of Hallelujah Chorus he stood up to give the King of King's homage and honor. Everyone followed the royal protocol by also standing to their feet. The impact of this work still being performed over two hundred and seventy years later around the world is immeasurable. It continues to bring people to their feet in awe of its message and power primarily because a devoted friend visited Handel in his despair, and was a vessel of encouragement that launched him into his destiny to impact generations to come.

Thank you, Charles Jennens, for having an ear and a

tongue to sustain the weary. Is there a depressed "Handel" in your life? You may be the one catalyst for his or her future accomplishments. Your words and assistance might be just the impetus needed to set this person back into orbit.[12]

Is there a depressed "Handel" in your life? You may be the one catalyst for his or her future accomplishments.

E-Mail = Encouragement Mail

I received an urgent email to pray for a dear friend's daughter just diagnosed with thyroid cancer. The next morning I listened with my heart to the Sovereign Lord for any "messages to share" and was reminded of a specific verse of scripture that I *knew* was for my friend and her daughter. Knowing and having memorized many

1. https://www.christianitytoday.com/history/people/musiciansartistsandwriters/george-frideric-handel.html
2. https://www.mormontabernaclechoir.org/messiah/george-frideric-handel-a-brief-history.html

scriptures is a significant asset to this process. Now I needed to act and deliver. It took only a matter of seconds to get up and send the following short email to my friend in Tennessee:

Dearest A, M, and R,

A scripture the Father has highlighted for you:
"For the eyes of the LORD move to and fro throughout the earth that He may strongly support those whose heart is completely His," 2 Chronicles 16:9.

He is strongly supporting you, A, M, and R this day!

Love,

Claudia

A wrote back:

"Ahhhhh! Thanks for that encouragement this morning. I awoke this morning and didn't want to get out of bed, but my thoughts were so scary that I couldn't stay in bed. I got up and fixed my eyes on Jesus, and the peace returned. I treasure your words to me today.

A"

Later, I received an email back and learned that R had recently endured a broken engagement, just weeks before the wedding was to occur. About a week after the broken engagement, the doctor diagnosed thyroid cancer in a lump on her neck. On top of this, her older sister, also her closest friend, was heading off to college far away.

"R and I were crying on the couch this afternoon after her sister drove off to move to Nashville. R said, 'I don't think I want to live. There is nothing left.' I started praying because I could see why she was feeling that way. As I prayed, the Lord told me to take her to your email. Then her whole countenance changed, and she was ready for the next step. Thanks. Over the miles, the Lord used you mightily. Thanks. I am deeply grateful.

Love,

A"

> *Jesus knew, ahead of time, that these ladies would be dismayed and very "weary and ready to give up" that day and wanted them to have something from Him to sustain them.*

Jesus knew, ahead of time, that these ladies would be dismayed and very "weary and ready to give up" that day and wanted them to have something from Him to sustain them: to uphold, support, and encourage them to carry on, to keep going. It moves me deeply when I think of how intimately our Sovereign Lord is acquainted with all our grief and how very personally and passionately He wanted to manifest Himself to those two women weeping on their couch. He looks to and fro for anyone whose ear and tongue might be available to Him so that He can break into this world to reach us when we are losing our grip. It underscores to me the great honor and responsibility He has entrusted us to be His lifting-up vessels on the earth. After all, it was a simple email that took seconds to send.

I heard again from A telling me of the upcoming radiation treatment R will endure:

"The isolation will last 1-5 days determined by how long she stays radioactive. The radioactivity is on some iodine which all remaining thyroid cells will drink up, so this treatment does not affect the rest of her body. Please pray to that end.

She was to get married the next week so as you can imagine the additional difficulty of going through that loss, coupled with being at Vanderbilt Hospital all week, all alone. Please pray for that time. As a mom, I can hardly think about it. Oh, Claudia. Her heart will be completely His. Your verse has been our theme. Thanks. Thanks for your loving concern and all the prayers. I send my love to you over the miles and thank you for loving me."

With His love,

A"

I inquired how everything went, and this is A's answer:

"Praise His Holy Name. We got the body scan back last week, and the treatment was in her body long enough to go to where it needed to go. The other good news. It doesn't look like there was any spreading. Your word to her...' Strongly support those whose heart is totally His'...yes, that has been the testimony here. She has known that she doesn't have to DO anything to be totally His...She is that. Oh, joy. And His strong support has been genuine and dramatic. I can't thank you enough for your help to me and her during this time.

With His love,

A"

This story is just one small example of how a little God-inspired, simple, e-mail or text of encouragement can travel a very long way. This family lived on the hope and promise of that one verse from His throne. Years later, R is happily married, with three beautiful children. Thanks be to God.

"He who spreads sunshine into the lives of others cannot keep it from his own."

Start a Tsunami Today!

Try An Encouragement Experiment

I guarantee that over time, we can change the atmosphere of our home or place of study or business with simple words of encouragement. This is not a gimmick, but a valuable exercise in learning how to love people in word and deed. It must always come from a sincere desire to care for people and then to sensitively communicate kind and truthful affirmations.

Plant flowers in others' gardens and your life becomes a bouquet!
-Author Unknown

Start with an intentional and sincere compliment of someone in your home. Watch their shocked or blushing expressions, and you'll know you've hit a chord. Like a pebble thrown in a lake, the ripples of those kind words will spread. Continue spreading this contagious encouragement virus at the office, at home, with friends. Purposely accentuate the positive in the people you encounter and in each situation you face. It may be the only kind word they hear all month.

Begin taking note of admirable things in the lives of those around you. Many times we have noticed qualities we admire but never get around to expressing those sentiments. Maybe a co-worker is usually cranky but always gets the job done. Express thanks for that. Perhaps a boss is generally so self-absorbed, he or she rarely notices the hard work going on around the workplace, but is always there early trying to solve problems. Choose an appropriate moment to express your thanks for having a boss who is diligent and cares about the business.

Think of a way to bless the staff at your employment and bring in a bouquet or some delicious chocolate. Attach a note that says, "You guys are an awesome staff!" or some such kudos. Though you may not see it instantly, know that you are making a difference in an entire group's morale.

More extroverted personalities can expand uplifting remarks to include encouraging strangers we encounter throughout the day. A smile and warm-hearted word to the postal worker, the clerk at the grocery store, or the jogger passing by can become their highlight in an otherwise drab or depressing day. Intentionally hold open the door to a public place and let others go first. Shocked by this very minuscule but significant gesture of kindness, people brighten up and for a second, may feel that they matter. They do matter ...enough for Jesus to die for them.

Reflect on the impact of your words. Your very words have created smiles, blushes, hope, and even a lingering joy in the people in your path. Whatever silver boxes you give to uplift others are bound to come back someday. But knowing you were a conduit of love to others is payment enough. "He who spreads sunshine into the lives of others cannot keep it from his own."

It is my goal, from my morning "listening time," or as the day unfolds, to receive a few names to encourage each day. If I was faithful to encourage just three a day, it would impact 1,095 people a year. If only ten others did the same, 10,950 individuals a year would be affected. If a thousand world-changers read this and spread the wave of encouragement, 1,095,000 people a year would be strengthened to carry on. No doubt, each of those revitalized ones would naturally spread that same words of cheer, and the repercussions could be immeasurable. It costs so little, but it precipitates *so* much UP life.

Start your creative encouragement wave today. Start with just one person a day and see how smiles bloom. Let no one you have encountered throughout the day leave without feeling a little lighter. Love picks up others... one word, one prayer, one deed at a time. Leave *your* God-imprint on hearts forever. In reality, the body of Christ is the dwelling place of Jesus for others to see. We dive into more uptrends next.

I love and include here the lyrics to the final song in the movie UP.

Life's a balloon

That tumbles or rises

Depending on what is inside

Fill it with hope

And playful surprises

And oh, dearie ducks

Then you're in for a ride

And there's nowhere to go but UP!

BONUS BOOSTER

Although our physical bodies are living on earth, spiritually, we are seated with Christ as UP as one could ever be!

"I have been crucified with Christ. It is no longer I who live, but Christ who lives in me." Galatians 2:20

Small-Group Discussion – Journal Questions

ELEVEN: LISTEN UP and LIFT OTHERS

1. Read Isaiah 50:4 together. Review how this invitation reveals the heart of God.

2. What is the role of the ear? The tongue? The action?

3. Share a time when you have experienced hearing something for another person and then sharing it. What were the results?

4. Think of several times you can see Jesus operating in this ministry.

5. Take a little time in prayer right now to listen and jot down names or impressions.

6. Next time you get together, share stories of how you listened and spoke into a "weary" one's life.

13

HOW TO SHOW UP AND BE JESUS "WITH SKIN ON"

When you get there, God gets there.
-T. L. Osborn

There are many times when the best and only way to impart strength to someone is by simply showing up. The ministry of *your presence alone* can speak volumes. There is a poignant story of a child who was afraid of the thunder at night and kept running into his parent's room for comfort. They would give him a hug and tell him, "Go back to your room, now, Jesus is with you." This scene repeated three more times and when the parents started again to tell him that Jesus was with him, he cried out, "I *know* Jesus is with me, but sometimes I just need somebody with skin on!" Don't we all?

It is hard to determine who gets the most benefit when we show up to express love...the givers or the receivers. The answer is both. This explains what Jesus meant when He said that it was *better* to give than to receive. The spiritual joy that fills us when investing in others refreshes our *own* soul, and then we have more to give. Love becomes its own reward. When we are living out the greatest commandment to love others in the same way that He first loved us, we experience the peak satisfaction of His endless flow of life into and through us.

This reality can create an exciting atmosphere for a team effort when a group of believers decides to rise up together to meet a need. This is the essence of true ministry: loving the world with the grace and presence of Christ which has been infused in us. We cannot export what we

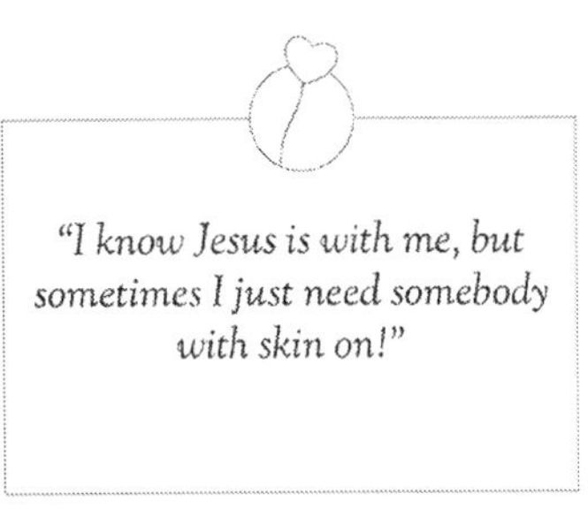

haven't imported. Learning to receive His power of encouragement is not only for our benefit, but can then bring benefit to the lives of others. When He fills our cup to overflowing and we have the privilege of sharing that infusion, there is nothing on earth more satisfying. 2 Corinthians chapter 1, verses 3 and 4 transmit this timeless truth. "Blessed be the God and Father of our Lord Jesus Christ, the Father of compassion and the God of all comfort, who comforts us in all our troubles, so that we can comfort those in any trouble with
the comfort we ourselves have received from God. "

Here is a true story of being moved by compassion into action and intentionally planning to "show up." This Columbine team shared the comfort they had received in their excruciating fire with students in Germany recently baptized with the same fire. Oh, the magnificent power of just being Jesus "with skin on" for someone in a time of desperate need.

News of the horrendous school shooting in Erfurt, Germany came not too long after the heart-wrenching impact of the tragic shooting at our local Columbine High School. On the evening of the Columbine shooting of 12 innocent lives, my husband and I were called to the auditorium where only parents whose children had *not* returned on the buses waited anxiously. A member of our church had called us to come and we stood weeping with the understanding that her child most likely would not return.

As a community, we walked through the depths of anger and agony while grieving the loss of twelve young students and a teacher. This story of God's miraculous healing and help in this desperate time of need is found in my husband's book, *The Martyrs Torch.*

Over time, having received God's inflow of comfort and strength through that crucible, our Torchgrab team of youth wanted to pass on that restoring comfort to help those suffering in Germany. We bought plane tickets and contacted local believers in Germany who also wanted to join in the mission and helped arrange things for us to visit this traumatized city and nation. Miraculous moments unfolded.

The Medieval Town of Luther Shocked by Mass School Shooting

Tears filled the eyes of our German breakfast waitress in our hotel when she learned why we had come all the way from Littleton, Colorado to Erfurt, Germany.

"We are a group of surviving students and friends and family members of the slain in the Columbine school shooting," I revealed, "here to offer comfort to your community."

"We...*know* what you are going through," I shared, referring to their recent horrific school massacre, April 26, 2002, at the Johann Gutenberg School. A 19-year-old former student, snuck in with a 9 mm pistol, dressed in all black and a ski mask and fatally shot thirteen teachers, two teen-aged students, a police officer, and then killed himself. Just days before we had arrived, tens of thousands of mourners had filled the town square on the steps of the ancient medieval cathedral to grieve this unprecedented act of violence that had ravaged their lives.

"My niece, Inga, witnessed that angry student when he shot her teacher to death at school that fateful day. She still cannot eat or sleep well," she said in a soft voice, wiping tears with her brown, calico apron. The lines on her forehead and her disheveled, auburn hair revealed her own tired features.

"Please tell her that students and friends from the Columbine school tragedy have traveled from America to meet her. We understand what she is going through. If she wants to talk, she and any of her friends are welcome to come to our hotel here tonight," I implored, amazed at how quickly this divine connection came about within just an hour of arriving. We had no way to get the names or phone numbers of these traumatized young people....We had simply flown in faith to their quaint medieval city where Martin Luther once preached in 1501, believing that we would be directed to them in some way. Love would find a way.

Tears erupted into sobs as our waitress fled out of the room to compose herself and call her niece. That one phone call and a front-page article in their German paper about our "mission of mercy" caused dozens of teens reeling in grief from this fresh tragedy to come out of the woodworks to find us.

Word spread like fire to these broken high-school students and teachers that a group had come from Colorado to express sympathy and compassion. We placed two six feet wide floral wreaths of gorgeous gold and purple flowers on the steps of the Gutenberg school. The burning candles and clumps of bouquets were reminiscent of the Columbine memorial displays. "Mit Liebe Aus Littleton, Colorado," or "With Love From Littleton, Colorado," the white satin sash draped across these giant floral symbols of sympathy read.

The officials of the schools would not sanction any official meeting, stating that their young people "did not need any outside help." The students knew differently and came by the dozens to seek us out late at night in our modest used-to-be East Germany hotel.

"Are you sent by some American business or government corporation?" Friedrich, a tall blonde student asked, representing the group of six somewhat reluctant girls and guys and an older woman standing behind him.

"*No*. We all paid our own way with the help of some of our friends in America just to try to bring you a little comfort," I answered, amazed at the suspicion. Friedrich translated for those who did not understand English as well.

Their eyes widened in unbelief, "THANK YOU...we... don't know what to say..." several replied. Visibly shaken, two blonde girls with nose and lip piercings embraced and began to cry.

"Please, have a seat here, and let's learn one another's names," Bruce remarked, trying to make them feel comfortable. "I am Felix, this is Marta, Heidi, Hans, Agnes, and Markus..." and the conversation was on.

"My favorite art teacher was gunned down at my feet," mumbled Marta, with dyed black hair, squirming in her chair, "she was one of my best friends."

"I looked out in the hall and saw my history teacher on the ground. I thought he was just playing dead as a joke until I bent down to talk to him and saw the blood gushing out of his mouth," remarked Hans, a 16-year-old, blonde boy, catatonically.

"We were hiding for hours in our classroom, all huddled together, listening to the screams and gunshots just outside our doors...we couldn't get to the bathrooms," Heidi, a younger girl, cried passionately, reliving the traumatic moments.

"I've been on the faculty here for twenty years," an attractive, petite, short-haired teacher of Literature relayed softly and reflectively, "I lost a dozen of my closest colleagues in one day....I've been to twelve funerals in the last few weeks," her voice broke..."Why am I still alive?"

We listened to them. We wept with them. They released their pent-up grief freely in a safe place of understanding and love. They asked to hear our stories. Beth and Dana, the mother and sister of 17-year-old Rachel Scott, a victim of the Columbine shooting, shared their horrendous experience of losing their precious daughter and sister, the first to be shot down by one of the murderers. Columbine High School students on our team tearfully opened their freshly healing wounds to share and relive their nightmares of hiding under library tables while their friends beside them were slaughtered before their eyes. Mutual sobs and then silence punctuated our time. There was a holy exchange of "knowing" similar suffering that bound us all together as one.

The natural questions followed.

"How did you get through the pain, the nightmares?"

"How long did it take you to want to live again?"

"I feel guilty that I am alive...did you feel that way, too?"

The natural answers (or non-answers in some cases,) shared in this sacred meeting of open, shredded hearts came flowing out immersed in tenderness and sensitivity. "It was our relationship with Jesus that got us through and still gets us through the heartache. Without Him, we could not have made it. He carried us through every step and stage of our grief," Rachel's mother, Beth, shared in her soft and compassionate way, passing around a picture of Rachel for everyone to see. The sincerity of her mother's heart and words penetrated deeply.

By the end of our week, while sharing our terrible true tales, strong coffee, and Kuchen (German chocolate cake), these self-proclaimed atheists had noticeably softened their party line. They kept inviting their friends to listen and partake in this healing interaction of compassion. We became friends in affliction, acquainted through grief.

On our last evening, we issued invitations to the community for a public expression of solidarity. We gathered in the very old, ornate high school auditorium with dark paneled walls and stained glass windows, a befitting setting for what would transpire. Students and now families and people from the community were arriving and how shocked we were to see the floor *filled* with people we had fervently prayed would receive comfort for their wounded souls.

A middle-aged, gentleman shyly approached me, very reverent in his demeanor. “I am William Brown. My wife, Helga, was one of the teachers who was murdered. I have written a song in her memory. May I have the honor of playing it for you?” he asked with eyes markedly red.

“I am very sorry for your loss,” I emoted, “and it would be a great honor for us and to her for you to play your composition for us.” We welcomed our guests and then signaled to William to come. He slowly walked to the piano and introduced the song written for and dedicated to his late wife. “My wife loved teaching because she was passionate about her students. We...will never forget her,” he said with sincere admiration. A blonde girl, maybe thirteen years old, was clinging to him, keeping her hand on his shoulder as he tried to compose himself before starting. “That’s the daughter,” a student next to me whispered into my ear.

His haunting and beautiful composition to Helga filled the room and released more tears from us all. We felt like we were in an inner sanctum. No one wanted to break the sacred silence that followed when he completed his memorial tribute. When he was able, he stood and bowed, signifying that we could break the silence with our applause. I will never forget the beauty of that moment, and the sight of Beth and Dana going over to hug this special father and daughter. Never.

Next, our multi-talented team presented a seamless, spontaneous program of guitar compositions, poems, intimate and tear-filled stories of their journey to healing, a mime that Dana Scott performed in memory of her sister, Rachel, and a powerful, multi-media, dramatic dance choreographed to present hope in the midst of tragedy. The climax was lighting the Memorial Torch, an Olympic-sized gold torch, engraved with all the names of the victims at Columbine High School. This very torch with its brilliant flame had been gripped by hundreds of thousands of youth around the world, pledging to counteract violence with love and compassion. Now the invitation to lay a hand on it and "take up this torch of love" and meet the One who would heal their hearts was given to those attending, victims of the cruel pain inflicted by hate and violence.

I could *not* believe my eyes as they opened. The entire front of the auditorium was filled with students and families who were responding to this call. There were more rushing forward than in the entire rest of the auditorium. Our team formed a circle around them and together we melted into a giant huddle of crying and celebrating human beings, most of who were meeting their loving Creator and Savior for the first time. As this wedding of broken hearts to the Healer continued, I witnessed a new look in many eyes: it was hope. We passed the glowing torch carefully from hand to trembling hand. No one wanted to leave. We lingered long in the afterglow of love.

No longer the strangers and confessing atheists we met a few days earlier, they had seen a glimpse of Love with skin on, *our* skin. And that made all the difference.

Savoring our last breakfast in the hotel restaurant, Ingrid, the Auburn waitress we met before, rushed over to us, much more like an old friend than the reserved woman we had met that first day. "My niece is eating and sleeping now! Her heart is so much better," she reported enthusiastically. "We are so very grateful," her voice broke as emotion welled up and tears splashed down her cheeks, "that you came to us."

And so were we...so were we.

Praise be to the God and Father of our Lord Jesus Christ, the Father of compassion and the God of all comfort, who comforts us in all our troubles ***so that we can comfort those in any trouble with the comfort we ourselves receive from God.*** *For just as we share abundantly in the sufferings of Christ, so also our comfort abounds.* 2 Corinthians 1:3-5 (NIV)

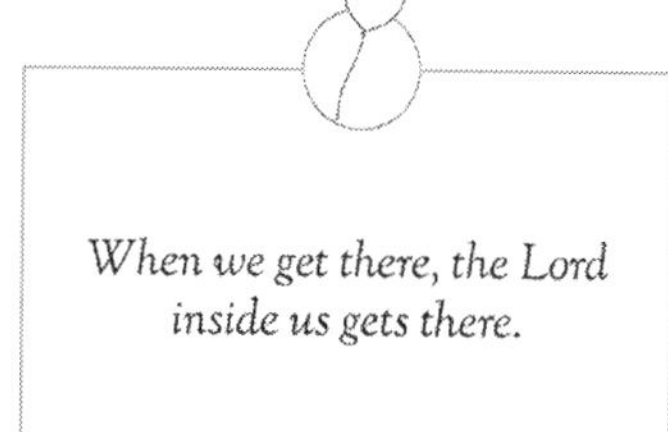

This next story also beautifully illustrates the joy of being vessels of encouragement, Jesus "with skin on."

Tissues for Our Tears

A Divine Encounter in Vienna Singing to Refugees Escaping ISIS

Choirfire is a music school and ministry I founded and direct (www.choirfire.org). My passion is to harness the power of children and young adults singing beautiful songs of good news as another way to release the outflow of encouragement to all who hear. I call it training and sending "Musicianaries" out to bless the world. This story is one of many exemplifying the power that flows when we "show up" to lift others.

The suffering in this world overwhelms me. I watched the news and saw the ghastly images of total devastation and the desertion of whole neighborhoods in Syria. I felt so much compassion. "Please, Lord, if there is any way that my life can help even one of those displaced millions, here I am." He would take me up on that prayer.

Excitement spilled over as my troupe of Choirfire singers

prepared to travel to the International Choral Festival in Vienna. We had practiced our Mozart and Handel and many glorious songs to perform in the great halls of the City of Gold.

On the way to the airport, I heard the news that thousands of refugees fleeing Syria were going to be streaming through Vienna and into Europe the *same* weekend of our visit. Struck by the non-coincidence of it all, I had a sense that somehow this was a divine setup.

My ensemble of mostly teens marveled at the elegance of Vienna, savoring a short cruise down the Danube, visiting famous composer sites and museums, and singing in schools and at the festival concerts. While touring the spectacular Schoenbrunn Palace and gardens, I asked our guide where we might encounter the incoming refugees from Syria. "We do *not* have any such refugees arriving," she barked. Back at our hotel, I asked the receptionist if she would check the local news and inform me of where there might be refugees entering. She reported that they were pouring by the thousands into the main train stations.

I gathered my team of singers and told them the news. "Let's bring our concert to welcome them," I proposed. "It is no accident that these dear people fleeing their war-destroyed homes are passing through the city we are in on the *very* weekend we are here!" They agreed to cancel the day's grandiose sightseeing plans. We headed to the subway that would take us to the downtown railway station. "This is what you call being a true musicianary, guys. Imagine what horrors these children have seen and the fear they all must feel," I shared.

Piling off the train into the station, we squeezed through the congestion of people and planted ourselves a few feet from the throng of arriving refugees who were moving toward the next train platform. Choking on the pungent smoke, we whispered a prayer and began to lift our voices and violin in hope-filled songs of welcome. The surprised and grateful looks and sweet personal nods from even the police energized us. A little girl in a red bandana was looking back and forth at her mother who was intently listening to us sing "Amazing Grace" while secretly wiping her tears. Her daughter smiled and waved as they moved along in the line as if to thank us for helping her mommy with our songs.

> *"While I was listening to your group singing, I had a strong feeling that you could tell me who the man in white is in my reoccurring dream."*

A comfortless, unending parade of exhausted young mothers passed by carrying crying newborn babies in one arm and what appeared to be all their worldly possessions in one trash bag in the other. Brave fathers transported their children piggy-backed and drooped over their shoulders while trying to keep their relatives together in the commotion. Older sons carried poorly wrapped bundles of all they had left in this world.

We stood amazed watching the universal love language of music cut through cultural barriers and transfer a measure of tangible love and strength to help them in their tragic trek. Seeing the fatigued faces and thankful eyes gazing into ours as we presented our gift of song, emotion overwhelmed us. Some of them had the presence of mind to notice the unstoppable tears escaping from our eyes and came over to offer us *their* tissues for those tears. Here we had come to comfort them, but they were comforting us! Greater sobs resulted.

While taking a break for water, a local man from a charity invited us upstairs to a room his organization had created to give rest to the families waiting for their departure, specifically for their children. Every kind of toy, doll, and craft decorated the floor for the littlest ones to enjoy. Carts of water and food, as well as all sizes of shoes and clothes, were provided for all.

"Sing here, for the children!" the leader implored. We eagerly lined ourselves up and joyously sang. One of our singers pulled out his juggling balls and further entertained our wide-eyed watchers. We played with the beautiful, black-eyed boys and girls who were a little shy at first. Smiles broke free as we blew bubbles, colored pictures, and played guitar, and games. I couldn't help noticing their parents' expressions of relief that their traumatized children finally were experiencing moments of childlike joy. Our hearts brimmed over with love and thankfulness for the opportunity to touch these beloved lives.

Returning to sing in the pandemonium below, a dark-skinned man stepped out of the crowd and asked to speak with me. Ibrahim was Syrian, ethnically Yazidi, and told me that he had fought in the army against Isis. He showed me a photo of his car business, now destroyed. Then he sighed as he turned to a photo of "my wife and child who were killed by a car bomb." I just listened, trying to process his calamity.

He was waiting for his mother and brother to arrive today to begin a new life together. Ibrahim politely asked me about something that had been plaguing him for decades. "While in Syria, I had a recurring dream for many years. In this dream, a man in white would stand at the end of my bed and beckon to me. Then he would disappear. Night after night, year after year, this dream bothered me. A few years ago during the war, the dream stopped. But suddenly, after arriving here a few days ago, it came back. While I was listening to your group singing, I had a strong feeling that you could tell me who the man in white is in this reoccurring dream."

I was speechless, struck by the significance of this divinely directed encounter. "The man in your dream is Jesus Christ, the Son of God, who came to earth, died on a cross in Jerusalem two thousand years ago for your sins, and rose again from the dead. He is the Savior of all who believe and trust in Him. He wants you to know and follow Him. You can read all of this in the Bible." He nodded slowly and declared, "Thank you. I believe what you say is the truth." Whistles blew, and police directed the crowd onward. He disappeared with them.

Paralyzed by the magnitude of this exchange, I tried to grasp the impact of this sovereign experience. My group of singers from Colorado took a divine detour from our fancy, festival itinerary and got to meet and share a sprinkling of comfort with some of the afflicted ones for which I'd prayed. And He had even let me interpret a heavenly dream, solving a life-long spiritual puzzle for a sincere seeker who had never read a Bible or heard the wonderful story. A truly miraculous encounter for us all.

It wasn't singing in lofty cathedrals or palaces, or cruising the Danube that we remembered most about our time in Vienna, but the tear-stained, appreciative faces we serenaded and encouraged for a few steps of their difficult journey. My forever-changed singers had experienced the *greatest* joy of being His hands and feet overflowing with the love of Christ to these strangers. They realized the power of lifting others up through the power of His encouragement inside them.

We don't need to wait for a dramatic disaster or headline event to be a part of a supernatural encouragement mission. Every day there are opportunities to hold a hand, take a walk with a despondent friend, visit a neighbor who is sick, or attend an important gathering for a cause. When we get there, the Lord *inside us* gets there. And what more powerful visitation could there be? Jesus in your skin and mine!

The transforming tools for living UP are ours. The undercurrents of doubt and hopelessness that surround us, forever seeking to pull us toward a vortex of negativity and resignation have *no* power over us. Let's *refuse* to be a victim of mediocrity, *rebel* against those destructive tides and downward spirals, and every day, every hour, determine to live UP by the continual inflowing power of His encouragement. We *have* spirit-infused power to venture, withstand opposition and take courage for the upstream voyage toward our God-inspired dreams. It doesn't matter where we start, just that we *do* start.

One by one, thoroughly embrace these dynamic truths. Get some friends together to wrestle with the discussion questions included. Begin your adventure toward supernaturally living UP, always looking for opportunities to lift others along the way. Soon, you will have your *own* miraculous stories to tell. Just keep plumbing the depths of your union with the greatest Encourager of all and walking out these ten catapulting truths.

1. OPEN UP to love.

Stop that resistance reflex to encouragement. Author

2. CLEAN UP your false identity tattoos.

The soul is dyed the color of its thoughts. Heraclitus

3. HOOK UP to Encouragement Himself.

Face every challenge connected to Diety: the Holy Spirit. Author

4. KEEP UP when you feel like giving up.

Nothing great is ever achieved without much enduring. St. Catherine of Siena

5. FILL UP with the creative power of His joy.

Stop postponing joy! Author

6. STAND UP and let your heart take courage in the face of ravenous attacking lions.

Courage is fear that has said its prayers. Dorothy Bernard

7. How did Joshua STAND up?

A champion is someone who gets up when he can't. Jack Dempsey

8. CHEER UP even when you feel alone.

Learn the vital art of encouraging yourself! Call, Remember, and Praise. Author

9. How Did Jesus Encourage Himself on the Cross?

Know who you are as revealed in God's Word! Author

10. PRACTICE UP and lift others daily.

Learn the vocabulary of encouragement and practice daily. Author

11. LISTEN UP and lift a sinking soul.

The Sovereign Lord has given Me the tongue of disciples,
that I may know how to sustain the weary one with a word. Isaiah 50:4

12. SHOW UP and bring His miraculous presence to the scene.

When you get there, God gets there T. L. Osborn

BONUS BOOSTER

God raised us up and seated us with Him in heavenly places:

"in order that in the coming ages He might display the surpassing riches of His grace, demonstrated by His kindness to us in Christ Jesus," Ephesians 2:6-7

For we are the product of His hand, heaven's poetry etched on lives,
created in the Anointed, Jesus,
to accomplish the good works God arranged long ago. Ephesians 2:10 (The Voice)

We are to be His kindness and grace on display for all to see. Reflections of His rich mercy toward us. His joy is our remarkable strength.

We can live with an eternal perspective as we walk through life seated "above it all" and filled with Him.

"He who sits in the heavens laughs," Psalm 2:4 We are sitting there, and we can laugh, too!

He laughs because He sees the end from the beginning. And we can, too.

Small-Group Discussion – Journal Questions

TWELVE: SHOW UP

Answer with a friend, a group, or individually in a journal.

1. Read Colossians 1:27. Based on this verse, discuss how God plans to get the glory that belongs to Him.
2. Read Galatians 2:20. Based on these two verses, what do you think Jesus thinks about the idea that we can be "Jesus with skin on."
3. Look over the table of contents and pick three chapters/topics that were the most impacting or helpful to your life. Share why.
4. Look back at your survey and analyze if you have already begun to change.
5. After reading this book, how do you plan to live your life a little differently?
6. Create a strategy to do this with friends and family to impact your world.
7. Consider gathering a group and leading this UP study with them.

Made in USA - Crawfordsville, IN
11907_9781732355743
05.31.2022 0949